Seasonal Occult Rituals

✛

William G. Gray

SKYLIGHT PRESS

© Marcia L. Pickands (estate of William G. Gray), 2014

Published in Great Britain in 2014 by Skylight Press,
210 Brooklyn Road, Cheltenham, Glos GL51 8EA

First published in 1970 by the Aquarian Press, London.

Designed and typeset by Rebsie Fairholm
Publisher: Daniel Staniforth
Cover art and photography by Rebsie Fairholm, incorporating a texture by
  Svenja Milautzcki

www.skylightpress.co.uk

Printed and bound in Great Britain by Lightning Source, Milton Keynes
Typeset in Prospero Pro. Titles set in Abdiel and Orpheus Pro.

British Library Cataloguing in Publication Data.
A catalogue record for this book is available from the British Library.

ISBN 978-1-908011-80-0

Publisher's note:
William G. Gray died in 1992. This new edition of *Seasonal Occult Rituals*, the first since its original publication in 1970, is sourced from the author's own 'correction copy' in which he had inserted some small text amendments. This edition therefore includes the author's intended corrections within the full original text.

Contents

✝

Seasonal Rituals

Seasonal Rituals

EASONAL rites are virtually as old as the hills they used to be practised on by most of humanity, and even today they are kept up in very attenuated forms by a small minority of cultists. In principle, they afford an invaluable means of aligning our own natures with the essential energy behind creation itself through the cycles and changes that complete the great circle of cosmos which we term simply 'nature'. Put into absolutely basic language, if we can find means of relating our little human nature with the incalculable divine nature, we shall have done something really worth doing. This was and is the aim of all true magical rites. To relate with the inside of nature, or the 'spirit within the stone'. To treat creation as an intelligent entity which knows very well what it is doing, even though we are yet unable to comprehend its type of consciousness. Not to give this inconceivable being the benefit of the doubt, but to obtain for ourselves the benefit of our belief in its beneficence. No inconsiderable advantage to us in such a transaction!

Thousands of years of human experience on earth have enabled us to relate ourselves to the natural physical properties of our chemical constituents, some of the inner forces immediately behind material manifestation, for instance electricity, magnetism, light, and we have discovered how to use most of our earthly environmental influences to our advantage – or otherwise. Why? Because in the first place our enquiring ancestors sought the inner spirits of these very matters, and successfully established sufficient contact with those categories of consciousness to hand them down through the ages, until they have become the heritage we treat so casually today. How did our early seekers manage this? By means of the ritual patterns they used as symbols for projecting their own inner intelligence into the state (or sphere) of existence beyond all their ordinary sensory information, and for obtaining the necessary enlightenment to justify and encourage their continued probing of consciousness at such an unusual depth. By looking for what might be called the soul of nature, mankind has eventually found out many secrets about its body. Maybe this has taken a long time historically, and undoubtedly we are still a long way from learning all there is to know in our cosmic corner, but unless we keep some sort of contact with the inside of our outside, we shall be in danger of losing touch with the only soul which might make our world worth living in – and then, we might as well all be lost.

It may be that we are falling away from the patterns of contact established by our ancestors because their external forms have become unsuitable for modern usage, and we have not as yet, in general, formulated any of our own along the same natural lines. This may be a pity, but it is not irremediable, and a sincere attempt at that very objective will be made in these pages. The four rites detailed have all been worked in practice by ritualists from several differing Western traditions, and have been proved quite successful during the years of their experimental trials. How they might work out over the larger field into which they are now being launched can only be shown by events. Either they, or the developments they lead to, will continue to serve human beings in search of their own souls and some meaning to their existence or not. If they even open up some practical way ahead to the light they are intended to reflect on earth, they will more than have justified themselves. Perhaps, to appreciate what lies behind them, we had better go back somewhat and trace the briefest possible line from their beginnings to their present appearance.

There is no particular mystery about the sort of rites our early ancestors used to work. With the twin fertility fluids of blood and seed, they laid the foundations of all future faiths on their ancient stones, which even now have stories to tell those with opened inner ears. Periodically, in accordance with the natural tides of nature and the times shown on the cosmic clock by sun and moon, the people came together in circles that symbolized their cosmic state, and there and then they made their dedicated representations of the things that bound them closest to the cosmic wheel of life. They did the things their concept of God commanded. They invited life among them by the only means available to them. They sacrificed a life from themselves in return. No ordinary, common life, but someone they genuinely loved, who cared enough for them to seek their welfare directly from divinity itself. Such a privilege belonged to royalty alone, and only royal blood could save the people. The King had to be sacrificed for all the others. Eventually this concept appeared as the mysterious 'Sang Real', or 'Holy Grail' (which only signifies 'Blood Royal'), according to which every member of humanity might ultimately be 'saved' through participation. So it continues today.

In addition to such sacred acts of life and death, the old ones acted out other incidents of the divine drama. They arranged their lives, settled their differences, put up their petitions and prayers, exchanged ideas, and in every possible way related themselves to their God and fellow men as best they might for all concerned. What more could they do? To what extent do we follow such a worthwhile scheme at the present time? Just how often do we make any real effort to align ourselves with the powers behind our presence in this world? Obviously we cannot very well, nor even should we, do the same things that took place so long ago, but the same principles provide the power behind the patterns and cycles of life in these days as in past ages. Force is eternal; only forms need altering.

With our modern record of bloodshed and sex, we are in no position at all to criticize the behaviour of early mankind, who was, after all, seeking to gain a soul rather than throw one away. Besides, who shall say that the old methods were entirely unsuccessful within the framework of living conditions at the time? We must remember that the original Sacred Kings were most willing victims in the name of their people, and they only quitted incarnation by everyone's common consent in order to link their souls with life on higher or 'heavenly' levels, from whence they might send back supplies of spiritual energy for the benefit of their old human families and friends. Moreover, they might ultimately reincarnate among those same folk during an act of ritual coupling, and so return once more to their people in human guise but with all the improvements they had acquired in the way of intelligence, character, and other spiritual faculties during their sojourn in celestial spheres. If such a process could be kept up long enough, man might develop traces of divinity on his own account, and the Blood

Royal be distributed through enough human families to secure its descent through the ages to come. Where would early humans possibly obtain such a sublime scheme, except by contact with a type of consciousness far greater than theirs in nature, which intended the ultimate union of mankind with itself in some common circle? Our distant ancestors acted in the best possible faith during their ritual patterns; these may seem crude to us now, yet they implanted the spiritual seeds in human nature from which we have grown to our present condition, such as it is, and upon which the fruits of our future depend.

Nevertheless, as man evolved, so did his power-patterns. Humans also ruined these for themselves by their own bad treatment of them. As the early rites degenerated into senseless orgies of slaughter and sex for motives of personal profit, so the spirit that originally inspired them had to find other ways of manifesting itself among mankind. The more advanced initiates responsible for the earthly components of the rites realized this very well indeed, and eventually managed to substitute animal for human sacrifice as a general custom, though not altogether, since human beings met ritual deaths in many instances for a long time to come. However, the pattern of progress was established whereby the more evolved human souls became, the less they should sacrifice their bodies in deaths dedicated to their deities. It was their lives on earth that were needed in service to the cause of cosmos, and this was the noblest offering to be made upon the altars of their faith. Instead of abandoning earth life and going out into the great unknown in search of that which they believed existed far beyond their bodies, humans discovered that it had followed them home, so to speak, and could now be met amongst themselves if they were prepared to recognize it, and knew how to look for it.

Had humanity learned its lesson the right way at that period of its history, we should have become much more advanced than we are at present. Unhappily, the fewer Sacred Kings were sacrificed in ritual circles, the more people were massacred in the inter-tribal murders of warfare. Instead of controlled breeding at definite seasons among those most suited to invite the best type of soul into incarnation, humans copulated with indiscriminate indifference to suit their immediate interests, and consequently peopled the world with those born of that same careless spirit. The peopling pattern intended to obtain the best results for incarnating entities in this world became hopelessly out of balance, and despite repeated attempts at stabilizing and restoring it to working order, its unstable and dangerous condition has shaken our history on its foundations. At present the degree of stability is so precarious that it needs a far deeper than average seer to predict the outcome with any certainty. The fate of the human race as a whole may literally be decided in a matter of a few minutes.

In order to lift the rites of basic human beliefs to higher levels of living, the original elements of flesh, blood, seed and sweat became symbolized by bread, wine, water and salt. The Holy Mysteries of old combined these into the most beautiful and uplifting liturgical formulae that might be devised by the mind of man inspired to express its entity through evolution. By no means all humans could accept this advance of awareness, some simply because they neither understood nor appreciated its necessity, but others for the really bad reason that it suited their motives of personal profit and power to encourage in everyone else the weaknesses and stupidities inherent in unselectively bred humans, so that the latter could be sold wholesale in the market-places of the world where mankind offers itself at a poor price to whoever can provide the showiest trade goods or apply the most powerful persuasions. The pattern of indiscriminate bloodshed and breeding for motives of profit and pleasure became too widespread and uncontrolled for any ritual regulation to be effective except on a temporary basis. Nevertheless such reformed rites were not without influence and effect altogether. At least they preserved and even promulgated correct cosmic patterns of procedure among selected initiates who might be trusted to hand these down their line of light to suitable souls who would in turn continue the tradition through every change in the cycles of the changeless circle.

At a later stage of development, more especially in the Western evolutions of the old Faith, the Christian Church attempted to incorporate and carry on the Mystery procedures and patterns. Because these were fundamentally sound in principle, they endured of themselves and carried the Church down the ages with them. Unluckily, the welter of dogmas, doctrines, obscurities, and all the rest of human mismanagement with which the Church authorities covered and confused the simple spiritual issues at stake, caused more harm than good over the ages. It is doubtful if any other major human faith can equal Christianity for mass slaughter and persecution of humans holding other beliefs. As an instrument of power politics, oppression, suppression of scientific enquiry, land and money-grabbing interests, the Church in general has been put to very bad use by those who took over its government for their own reasons. As against this, very many wonderful and devoted souls have found exactly what they needed among the traditional truths which the Church had formulated to suit itself, and so have been liberated into the light that all must reach to attain the Great Atonement (AT-ONE-MENT). True teachings exist in the Church as they do in any other body of belief, but it rests with the will of every single soul to go in and find that truth for itself The great difference between the Church and the Ancient Mysteries was and is that with the former, followers were told to take what was provided as it stood and be contently obedient, while with the latter, initiates were told to take the symbol-patterns they were given, and use these for making their own way along the path each of us must travel alone until we are able to atone (AT-ONE) for ourselves. The Church forbade individual liberty in light. The Mysteries were insistent on each initiate attaining Priest-Kingship for himself, and offered every inducement and encouragement to those attempting this cosmic course. Both Church and Mysteries stood for the same Ultimate, since there is but One for All, though their respective methods were so very different.

Although we talk about the 'Old Faith', and the 'New Dispensation' as though they were categories of human belief having nothing in common or any connection with each other, such is scarcely the case as seen by intelligent observers. Fundamentally our faith is one, and its variations are due to differences in the development of customs and consciousness by which we try to express it. Even if there were as many of these variations as souls practising them, they would all serve the same cosmic spirit, provided the intentions of the will were right. When we speak of 'Old' or 'New', therefore, we must realize that this refers only to an alteration of light-life levels in relation to our primal and perpetual problems of associating ourselves both individually and collectively with cosmos itself, and with the creative spirit which brings all to being.

Although everyone must relate himself with Cosmos in his own particular way, when it comes to a question of many people intending to acknowledge and extend this same relationship as a common or Group enterprise, some form of agreement obviously has to be reached among them. Time, place and event must be made to coincide for the occurrence to be relevant and so that all concerned may readily understand when it is, where it is and what it is. Hence the value of seasonal rites. Of old, everyone concerned would know well enough that the nature of the rite would be in keeping with the spirit of the season, it would be celebrated about the time of full moon, and it would be held on whatever hilltop was particularly sacred in the vicinity. Later of course, the venues changed to suit altered opinions or geographical necessities, and eventually the structure of the rites diversified to suit the different social, cultural and ethnical strata that have developed in the course of human history. If we are ever to arrive at a point of spiritual adulthood where we shall be fit to take our place among the Companions of Cosmos, we must clearly readjust our dislocated rings or circles so that some mutual means of correlating cosmos and our own consciousness may be found. In other words, we need some kind of rite in which those of differing personal and group systems can all participate and happily harmonize.

The Churches and established faiths of all categories have their own problems to work out along these lines, and most of their modern leaders are very well aware of what is involved. We are not directly concerned with them here except that our purposes are parallel. Divided as creeds may be, what could possibly be more split up than the descendants and inheritors of what we might as well call the 'old beliefs in the Inner Mysteries'? There is every reason why they should at present remain discrete from (and discreet with) each other, so far as their earthly and mortal manifestations are concerned, but at the same time there is a strong case to be made for even some simple ritual structure to be evolved whereby those in the various systems who are willing to work together along traditional lines might do so. What follows is the outcome of a trial attempt of this nature intended for Western workers

13

in particular, and anyone in general who feels he fits into the pattern.

At present the rites are limited to those four which are in keeping with the spirits of the seasons, and are celebrated at about the solstices and equinoxes. There is no hard and fast date or type of meeting place, this being left entirely to the convenience of those taking part. If possible, the nearest day to the full moon approximating the new season is a good time, but individual needs and availabilities will decide the issue. The basic pattern of the rite is the simple circle-cross of solar cosmos, and everything relates to its equatorial points and central pivot. There is no set size for the Circle, which must be determined by the number of people present, but since the maximum around the perimeter is ideally twelve, the Circle should not exceed the diameter needed for this number to face centre while holding each other's hands at arms' length. Actually that is the quickest and most sensible way to work out a circle for any number of people.

The direction of the rites falls principally upon the four Officers of the Quarters, who are simply designated by their position at East, South, West and North. They correspond of course to Elements, Instruments, and all other quarterly attributes. The action of the rite takes place around the circle which symbolizes the cosmic course, and everything taking place is in sympathy with whatever season is being entered in spirit as well as body. There is music, movement, meditation and meaning in the rites, which add up to magical procedures. A password for the period or key-phrase to use during the following three months is chosen, and the mood, determination, or will of all concerned at that particular time is set and dedicated. Divinity is recognized and honoured, while humanity relates itself with whatever is best of the two different states of consciousness attempting union of the ultimate circle.

Since the rites are designed for those of varying opinions and systems to work together, divine names, and other attributions to specialized branches of the Mysteries, are only made in the most general possible way. Probably one of the best backhanded compliments the rites were paid was a criticism intended to be caustic, that they were 'Much too Christian to please the pagans, and far too pagan to suit any Christian'. Actually there are no particular references to either of those systems, which are not nearly so far apart from each other as might be unthinkingly supposed. Although the importance of the rites lies in their patterns rather than their wording, the general plan of the script is to be simple; straightforward yet metrical, with sufficient dramatic content to make good hearing and feeling. A slightly unusual feature is the amount of free expression allowed to the officiants in the matter of consecrations and dedications. There is a special reason for this. It is presumed that at least the officers will be competent ritualists in their own right along the lines of whatever system they personally follow. Privately for instance, (as in the case of one circle) they might consist of a Celticist, a Qabalist, a Druid, and an Old Religionist (which last is not and never was associated with witchcraft). A curious combination which one would imagine a fairly impossible assortment of people, yet they settled down quite well to their mutual task, each using methods that came naturally to them for what they were, and these all harmonized very reasonably.

Should the officiants not belong to any established system this is probably more of all advantage than otherwise. Each will be responsible for constructing as necessary his own formulae for blessings and dedications, and he will have an entirely free hand in this matter. If what he does or says does not suit the others, this will undoubtedly become evident and there will be all opportunity for alteration during the next quarter. Each Officer has a Quarter of his own, during which he acts as principal for that ceremony and throughout the coming season. It makes a nice touch if some symbol such as a ring or banner is handed from one to the other as the year progresses. A collar of office is a very customary way of doing this, but any imaginative method is better than indifferent neglect.

The rites are not designed to 'start from cold', but to be preceded and terminated by whatever sort of lead-in and closure suits those taking part. This may be anything ranging from silent meditation to a musical overture and a short address of seasonal significance. A tape-recorder is an asset here, since this enables music and talk to be preset, and the talk might be given by someone not even physically present. Ideally, each Officer ought to be responsible for an address about the topic of the season, which should not exceed five minutes, or less if possible.

This is by no means an essential item, but can be helpful, providing it is purposeful, pointed and not unduly protracted. One useful opening procedure consisted of a few purificatory and dedicatory prayers, a symbolic procession around the circle, then the address followed by the opening music. Closure was effected by remembrances of the absent, the sick and the deceased, a petition for peace to all people, restoration of the symbols, and a final blessing followed by music. None of this took very long in the hands of experienced ritualists.

Choice of place will naturally be limited by the accommodation available. Open-air workings are very stimulating, but highly unreliable in European climates. Whatever place or room is finally chosen should be cleared as much as possible of unsuitable ornamentation and furniture, carpets, if valued, being best taken up unless a canvas floor-cloth with a circle design painted on it is available. Apart from easily portable symbols, there are few really solid accessories needed for these rites. A pair of plain black and white upright pillars are useful to indicate the Gate of the Quarter being approached, and the principal officiant will work between them. Failing this, any other symbolic means of Quarter Signs will serve. Garlands or floral decorations appropriate for the seasons are usually easy to make, and the meditation symbol is best contrived from such natural sources. Incense may be of a general type such as used in churches and temples, or specially designed to suit the season. It may be burned centrally on a small charcoal brazier type of censer, or if a proper thurible is used, this will be retained at the Southern point of fire.

If it is possible to arrange the circle so that its Quarters align with those of the earth, so much the better, but if not, 'magical' East will be wherever that Officer is positioned, and the others will group up accordingly. Unless considerable space is available, experience has shown the most practical seating to be comfortable stools, which are least likely to catch robes or cause damage if accidentally knocked. These may be pleasingly coloured to match the position or office of the occupant. Since each Officer has his proper permanent symbol of Sword, Rod, Cup, and Shield, there has to be some means of locating and displaying these during the rites. If they cannot be advantageously placed on the walls by each Officer, they can be put on small side tables which will be needed for such adjuncts as incense, elements, oils, etc, or if the worst comes to the worst borne throughout the rite by the Officers concerned. All these details have to be dealt with entirely according to the circumstances and those in charge.

Lighting presents its own problem. Since spring equates with dawn, summer with noon, autumn with dusk, and winter with night, it is well if such conditions can be simulated for the respective rites, no matter at what actual time of day or evening they happen to be held. Nevertheless there must be at least adequate lighting near each Officer for him to read his ritual script plainly. Even if such lights are small electric ones, there must always be a live flame in lamp or candle form by every Officer. Those with a turn for design may easily contrive symbolic candle or lamp holders to suit their intended positions in the circle. Traditionally, north has only a small flame in a blue glass to indicate starlight, but a reading light of some kind is an obvious necessity for that Officer.

The central or Solar Point around which the circle cosmates must have a flame of fire which will burn clearly and brightly enough for the circumambulations to be made around it. Again its precise nature varies considerably with circumstances, the risk of fire, etc. In the open, of course, it would present no particular problem, but naturally great care has to be taken indoors. One group solved this neatly enough by means of an old iron cauldron with a methylated camping stove inside on a half brick, and a sandfilled flowerpot which might be used as an extinguisher in emergency. There are many ingenious ways of working out the question of the central fire, but it cannot well be dispensed with on account of its vital symbolical importance. Even the smallest workable flame in the centre, capable of burning a few pieces of paper, will do, but its practical presence is absolutely essential. It is advisable to rehearse the fire factor very thoroughly indeed if the rites are to take place indoors, so that fuel may be calculated to the nicest degree. Methylated spirits are probably best for indoors since they make the least fumes. A home-made burner can easily be made from any suitable short tin and some asbestos string coiled flat in the bottom for one or two layers. Spirits are simply poured into this and ignited. About an egg-cup full will suffice. On no account whatever should paraffin or benzine be even considered as fuel for this essential fire. Better use a piece of solid fuel on an old tin plate and play safe than attempt some impressive effect that might end in tragedy, for an insurance company if none other.

The central flame kindled among the Companions of the Cosmic Circle does more than symbolize the divine light which they hope will come in the midst of them, both individually and collectively. It must consume their 'offerings', which take the practical form of papers on which they have written privately their personal and/or general summations concerning themselves and the seasonal spirit. This is a very important part of the rites. Indeed, and unless it is done conscientiously and thoroughly, the rites will lack an otherwise unobtainable quality. Whatever else may be abridged or altered, the presentation of petitions is morally obligatory for all who participate. Failure to do this indicates a serious lack of understanding as to the inner nature and operation of the rites, and anyone unwilling to take the necessary trouble to make out a petition properly is quite unlikely to benefit from them in any marked way.

What a petition really amounts to is facing oneself fairly and squarely in the spirit of the season, and having a private showdown on vital spiritual points which regularly need bringing to light. It is a question of realization and calculation rather than self-condemnation and meaningless regrets and repentance which do no good at all to anyone. What is needed most is a practical policy and some reasonable ideas for character alterations of which the petitioner is capable if given a fair chance. Should the competence seem evident, the chance to use it may justly be petitioned for. Suppose we consider the sort of petitions we might well present at the seasons.

Springtime is seed-time. If our souls were gardens, what would we like to plant in them? What qualities do we lack that we would be glad to obtain? Patience? Kindliness? Tolerance? No matter what it is, let it be noted, realized, and the small seed of an idea formed to that effect. In writing, it may be only, 'I need so-and-so. I will work for it. May opportunities be opened.' The shortest and briefest summations are always the best, providing they contain their meaning completely. Springtime is for new schemes, new ideas, fresh concepts. What comes to us? What would we will that might come to us? Whatever it is, let it be formulated and expressed. And why only for ourselves? Why not for others? Let us include their needs, too, in a seasonable way. We shall never reap a harvest on any level of life unless we first plant the seeds from which the fruits are likely to come, and spring is the occasion and opportunity for doing exactly this on our spiritual and consequently most important state of existence. Whatever it may be we want to grow into fruitfulness in ourselves or for others, spring is the right moment to call these seed-notions into the circle of our consciousness and reduce them to points of power to be implanted in the fields of inner energy.

Summer is the season for cultivation and caring. It produces flowers from which fruit must eventually form. As such flowers sustain us spiritually by their beauty and perfume in summer, so will their fruits sustain us substantially and physically later in the year. Now we have to face ourselves again in the magic mirror of our minds, and see just what we ought to cultivate in ourselves, what should be weeded out, and what has to be encouraged to better and fuller growth for what it will be worth in future. All this has to be sorted out, summarized, and made up on paper into a kind of periodic report on ourselves as though we were submitting a confidential memo to a superior concerning someone of whom we had charge. We do have such a charge of ourselves, and our spiritual superiors are entitled to receive reports about us from whatever source they choose. We also are entitled to submit our own estimates of ourselves for consideration.

In autumn, of course, the emphasis is on harvest. What have we done with ourselves during the year past that was worth doing? Just how many of our seed-ideas have come up, let alone produced any noticeable crop? Exactly what do we amount to in ourselves as humans, what might we be proud to say of, 'I grew that myself'? At this season of harvest in the spiritual year, what have we to show or know for anything we have worked on previously? Supposing we died physically at this instant, what spiritual harvest would we have reaped for the whole of a lifetime's effort which might sustain our souls until different sorts of natural support could be drawn upon? Very awkward questions these may be to answer honestly, but it is undeniably as well to face them at least once in a solar cycle. A human individual may be the richest person on earth as regards money or possessions, but the moment he quits his body, he is worth neither more nor less than the spiritual assets he has built into his inner identity, which survives separation from the flesh. Riches to rags in a flash for some souls, because they have so utterly neglected and despised the spiritual side of themselves. We are what we make ourselves or will to be.

The winter season has the unique property of being the best opportunity during the solar cycle for clearing away unnecessary debris, converting it into fertilizer, sorting out stock, burning off useless material, and generally preparing for fresh cycles of activity. Winter affords a chance for reflection, thinking things over, and considering future possibilities. What mistakes have we made in the past that we would rather not make again? What faults in ourselves would we be rid of? What is there in our lives which we might live better without? Undesirable contacts to be broken off? 'Dead wood' to burn up? Tidying up to do? Now is the chance for all this essential effort during the season ahead. Supposing we were dead, and given the privilege of getting rid of our past muddles and messes made during our earth-lives, straightening everything up in our souls, and clearly putting everything in ourselves into first class condition for starting our new life-cycles in the best conceivable way? What a possibility! Yet we are plainly offered the reflection of its equivalent on earth with every winter season, and how many of us really bother to use it? Who dares to say he would not be the better for a thorough spiritual clear-out and restocking at least once in twelve calendar months?

Such is the value of the petitions which should be burned in the fires of the quarterly rites. They should be the result of facing ourselves in the truest terms we can reach from four distinct angles of the solar circle. If we can manage to align ourselves with the central sun of spirit at least on those four occasions, in a manner corresponding with the season of cosmos we are passing through outwardly as earthly people, it will prove a very worthwhile relationship indeed. Why should we not acquire the ability to deal with life as it deals with us in a springlike, summerly, autumnal, and wintery way? This can be done if we word our petitions properly. How that is accomplished is a matter which everyone must discover for himself in practice. Self-analysis or estimation is never an easy task, and it must be remembered that this has to be done in four different ways, each with its own method of constructive suggestion. What we are really doing is to find and recognize the true wills that are within us, so that our inner and outer cosmos coincide in the most direct line of light we can make between the sun and the sun-behind-the-sun, as it were. Perhaps this may, and most probably will, take a lot of doing, yet it must be done.

However long it takes to come to terms with ourselves at the end of each quarter, the last thing to aim for is a sort of candid confession covering many sheets of script. It may be interesting to the person concerned, but it is useless for ritual purposes. What are needed are summations, and summations of summations, until, if possible, the whole issue is reduced to a few key-points covered in maybe one or two sentences which mean everything intended. If this might be expressed as a glyph or symbol, so much the better. Just as the entire transactions of a commercial company for a season might be summarized in a final financial figure which would indicate the state of the company to those understanding its significance, so should we be able to cast our spiritual accounts into a comprehensive representation easily appreciated by inner intelligence. This is what should be sought in formulating the petitions which are sacrificed in the seasonal flame of the rites. What really matters is all the work, thought and realizations that went into making them. If this is done properly, the right symbols should virtually suggest themselves.

If anyone has really serious difficulty in thinking out ways of making summations about the difference between what they are and what they will to be, a simple method is the good old 'quiz', or categorical questions. These may be of the 'yes' or 'no' sort to suit the seasonal spirit, and put into several groups under letter headings. Scores may then be added up, and combined to make the symbol of the petition, which would have meaning for the writer alone as a human, and otherwise for those or that it was addressed to. At least this is a convenient system, providing it is worked sincerely and not made into a mere grocery list like some boring chore. Whatever method is used to produce the final figure of a petition on paper, it should not be inconveniently large or over-bulky. A playing-card size is ample, and it can very well be smaller. No-one should attend a quarterly rite without this necessity having been fulfilled, and of course the petitions can be sent by proxy from those unable to be physically present.

Having thought about the seasons in a general way, let us consider what sort of people are most likely to typify or 'mediate' them individually as officiants of the Four Quarters. The best key to their natures is probably their symbolic instruments of Sword, Rod, Cup and Shield. These show the cosmic solar cycle in a very old traditional way, and indicate the kind of person best qualified to bear them.

In the East, associating with dawn and the spring season, the symbol of the Sword and element of Air are personified by Archangel Raphael. Here is needed ideally a young and highly intelligent male person, sharp and keen of mind and soul, quick-thinking, and alert for signs of trouble threatening the group from external sources. He is incisive and pliant, on the look-out for new projects or interests in which the group might engage if they decide to, and he keeps the rest very much on their toes by his enthusiasm and eagerness to get things right for them. Sometimes they may not be able to avoid an affectionate laugh at his enlivening spirits, which nevertheless keep them active and prevent complacency in the Cosmos all are trying to create together.

In the South, linked with noon and summer, the Rod symbol and dement of Fire personify in Archangel Michael. His human mediator should be the senior male of the group, who could be seen as a father-figure but is more of the commanding officer type. He upholds the conduct of the group, makes most of the rulings, keeps discipline, should set a good example, does the main job of straightening out problems affecting the group, and is perhaps the principal enlightener. He is responsible, with his opposite number, the Shield, for taking the chief decisions and judgments concerning group activities.

In the station of the West, connected with dusk and autumn, the beautiful symbol of the Cup and element of Water are personified by Archangel Gabriel (pronounced Jiv-ra-ee-el). The human representative here ought to be a young fertile (not pregnant) female. She mediates powerful and beneficial love and compassion throughout the group. If there should be trouble among them, her job is to mollify it, if sorrow, console the sufferers. She must be able to radiate cheerfulness, kindness, good humour and happiness from her Quarter. It is she that has to nourish (nurse) things along when they become difficult and, as Guardian of the Grail, keep in touch with the inner nature of this entirely sacred symbol.

At the Station of the North, linked with night and winter, the symbol of the Shield or Mirror and element of Earth are personified in Archangel Auriel (Au-ra-ee-el). Here the mediator should be the senior female of the group. She is the one of experience, wisdom, caution, tolerance, patience and all the qualities associated with good, sound, solid sense at its highest level in the human spirit. She helps to show people what they really are, and tries to protect them from over-impulsive propensities. She guards the traditions of the group, and teaches the law by which they hope to live.

One last symbol is worth mentioning, if any officer can be found to mediate it properly. This is the Cord, which should be a sort of universal link, able to operate as the periphery of the circle, join it with others, or connect any points within the circle. Such an invaluable individual, representing Archangel Savaviel, must be able to fill in any gaps with even minimal competence, fit in wherever necessity arises, contrive to tie things together that tend to slip apart, or act as a restraint to whatever goes astray in the circle, and generally be the faithful and indispensable dogsbody without which any human grouping whatsoever would infallibly disintegrate sooner or later. Circles having a reliable 'Cord' are very fortunate. The place of this Officer with the circle is wherever he may be needed. He is free to wander about the perimeter (always following the way of light) according to whatever may arise. The others must keep their Stations, except when circumambulations or processionals are called for, but the Cord is freely flexible in action. He carries symbols from one point to another, fetches whatever might be wanted, and operates as agent for any purpose. In other systems, he would correspond to the vital office of the 'Messenger' or Herald. He may, of course, be of either sex and any age at all, providing he is fit for his function.

As regards this question of functional fitness, it may well be that groups might find extreme difficulty in obtaining ideal types of officers. It should therefore be borne in mind that the nature of the office itself is of paramount importance over the purely physical characteristics of the human being needed to fulfil it. Providing a person is in himself fitted for some particular office, then he may certainly serve in that capacity regardless of age, sex, or other anomalies. So far as possible, every effort should be made to balance the offices of a group between the sexes and ages, because the principle of balance among a number of people around a central solar spirit is of primal necessity, but availability of material in human terms is an understood difficulty with all group workings of this kind. Sad experience has adequately proved that it is best not to attempt group rituals at all than work with unsatisfactory or totally unsuitable officers. Far more harm than good happens in such instances. In all instances of choosing officers, the individual characters and personal qualifications of the humans themselves must be considered first. Providing they are the sort of soul for the office they are best able to fulfil in relation to the others, their group will cosmate as well as any human association may be expected to hold harmoniously together.

This last point is worth consideration. Every normal person has some degree of all the Quarters in himself, since we are all miniature Cosmoi or microcosms in our own right. In relation to other humans, however, one Quarter or other usually predominates by reason of contrast to the rest of the group and that quarter therefore becomes the natural office which it is best for that person to fulfil for the benefit of the remainder. Thus someone making an ideal Rod in one circle might be best fitted for a Sword in another or even possibly a Shield in a third, though he is unlikely to make a Cup elsewhere. It all depends how souls relate with each other, and the essential thing is to associate in groups where harmonious relationships are possible between those who form its cosmic pattern.

Between the four Officers of the Quarters will be the other cosmic companions who complete the circle. These should on no account exceed eight (two between each Quarter), bringing the total present, including the Cord, to thirteen human people. The real thirteenth person of course is not human at all, but the presence of the power in the midst of them. Normally the companions will be deputy officers themselves, associating with one Quarter or another and taking their place in the circle nearest to their particular point of office.

It will be noticed, and should be emphasized throughout the rites, that the styles of address vary between sections: some are directed towards humans present and others towards the Inner Ones with whom spiritual contact is sought. The device of addressing these Beings as 'Thou' is adopted in order to distinguish between thoughts intended for direction to divinity, and those meant simply to be shared among intelligent human entities. This has proved a most useful idea in practice, since it enables consciousness to be shifted from one level to another with comparative ease. Some types of ritual employ alternations of prose and poetry or widely differing metres for this same reason, but an easy change of style works quite as well and is less troublesome to follow. With these seasonal rites, the whole trend and approach of each one is in accordance with the cycle being celebrated. In spring, the symbolic time of youth and childhood, the rite is almost childish in some of its language and terms. Summertime levelling with vigorous adulthood is spoken about from that viewpoint. Autumn, the season of fruitfulness and maturity (despite the preferably young Cup Officer), is dealt with in that sort of tone, and winter, the period of age and wisdom, is ritualized in a serious and quiet fashion. Thus, with the rites, we go through an entire natural lifetime in the course of a solar circle, and relate ourselves with Cosmos as children, adults, mature and old people, regardless of our physical age. Altogether they afford a means of making one life provide us with inner experiences and evolution which might otherwise take us many incarnations to achieve. That alone would be a sufficient reason for participating in these Quarterly Rites of the solar cosmic circle, although there is much more to be had from them by those who find out how to extract their deepest inner contents. Now let us look at the scripts of the rites themselves and see what these amount to.

✝

The Rite of Spring

✝

The Rite of Spring

There is minimum light, as at dawn. If humanly possible, this ceremony is best actually held at dawn. The companions are seated in their circle, silent and hooded as if in deep sleep. No sound but that of breathing. When the OFFICER OF THE EAST feels that the right moment has come, he rises, kindles the flame of East, sounds the Call to Life with pipe, syrinx or other wind instrument, then trips perimeter deosil, waking each companion cheerfully, returns to his Station, and declaims (as if to quite young people):

East: Awake! Awake! Awake! Awake! Return to life within this mortal world, O sleeping ones who wait rebirth from our Great Mother's womb.

Be born again with human hopes, O true companions of the cosmic light. The shining sun of spiritual strength and splendour wakes and welcomes you to life anew among mankind. Arise! Arise! Arise! you slumbering children of creation.

Here is Springtime, and the spirit of eternal youth unquenchably aflame for living and adventure! Accept it and rejoice! Time has turned full circle, bringing you to birth once more. You are young and fresh again, with every opportunity of life before you. Rise up and claim your birthright, take and use it faithfully according to the cosmic law,

IN PERFECT LOVE,
BE   WHAT   THOU   WILT.

Come into consciousness together, uttering the call of our creation.

I   A   O   M
(EEE)   (YAY)   (OOHH)   (HMMMMMM)

(This is the sound of a rising yawn, and also the name of arousing divinity.)

29

(All present repeat this vibrantly, rising, stretching arms, etc. as they come to order.)

South: Blessed be the light arising at our inner dawn to show the Way ahead upon our Paths.

(Lights taper from EAST, and illumines all other lights deosil, returning to Station.)

West: Blessed be the word of light above the waters of eternal life that brings us all to being.

North: Blessed be the light delivering our world from darkness and our spirits from despair.

East: Companions, it is good to be alive once more together, being as little children with each other, full of wonder and excitement with our new-found world. Why should we not enjoy this as all children may, with innocent delight and pleasure?

As we play our games of childhood, so shall we work as adults and evolve as individual souls. Everything arises from our primal patterns, and our best becoming follows on a true beginning. Therefore, if we set our pieces properly at first, the greatest game of life itself is bound to turn out well for us, whatever happens.

Let us try to put this pattern into practice here and now among us. Set up its symbols. Signify it joyfully with fresh fertility of mind and soul. Come forth from weary winter into glorious growing spring with gaiety and gladness. Look at life and laugh! Smile and sing together just because we are alive and full of energy that needs expression. Be happy for the sake of hope alone. To play and pray is one with every child of light. Do both together with a willing heart. Now!

(Here all decorate the place according to taste with spring flowers, garlands, personal adornments, or whatever has been decided upon. Cloaks and hoods, if worn, will be removed. Gay spring dance music played and perfumes diffused. However this may be done, the essential symbol for meditation later on, which must be some arrangement of an egg and seeds artistically combined, has to be either placed on the altar covered with a veil, or ready for production in some convenient

place of concealment. All this is done in the lightest-hearted way, there being no reason why people should not chatter and joke like children among themselves if they feel like it. When they are finished and back in their stations, the EAST calls them to order with three handclaps, as if they were children, and continues:)

East: As children of the Mysteries ourselves, we realize the power and possibilities of our imagination. Like play-pretence, our thoughts turn into things if we think hard enough for long enough. Let us imagine now that the divine ones, whom we honour in our hearts, are asking us what we would ask of them this coming season. How should we answer Them?

ALL: We do not know.

East *(cont.):* That is the truth. Of our own accord we do not know what may be best for us. Therefore in the spirit of sincere simplicity, like little ones that ask with fullest faith, let us approach our primal parents and implore:

O light divine, be thou our life, that we may learn thy law of perfect love, BE WHAT THOU WILT.

ALL: In perfect love, BE WHAT THOU WILT.

South: Yet suppose our own suggestions were made possible? What ideas among us should we bring to light this Springtime? What new notions have we to initiate and start upon their cosmic course? What sort of spiritual seeds do we intend to plant within us so that these may grow to beneficial fruitfulness for everyone concerned? This is the proper time to ask the Holy Ones for help with our endeavours to select and sow what must be rightly chosen and uprightly raised to light by all of us. Let us present our personal petitions to this purpose unto those whose certain aid we confidently ask this instant.

West: Who asks for nothing is already answered.

North: Who asks for everything receives the same reward.

East: Let us therefore ask no more than due fulfilment of our present needs as human souls upon our pathways to perfection.

(Here the petitions are collected deosil by SOUTH, and presented to EAST.)

South: On behalf of our companionship, both present and by proxy, I offer these, our hopes and prayers to the Eternal Ones that They may guide us safely through the gateway of our year ahead.

West: May our hopes be truly justified.

North: And may our prayers be heard indeed.

East: In the Name of the Great Germinator, and the spiritual cultivators of our inner fields, may these be accepted as good seeds for planting in the gardens of the soul, where also may they grow and flourish unto ultimate fulfilment as the fruit and flowers of our most fervent faith. Let their empty husks be burnt to fertilizing ashes by the blessed flame of light among us.

(Here SOUTH takes the petitions again, stacks them in brazier or equivalent, saying:)

South: Blessed be the gentle fire of spring that frees us from the frosts of winter and encourages our new activities.

(Here the OFFICER OF THE SOUTH lights the fire to burn the petitions, and blesses or consecrates it in whatever way he chooses. The form used is optional. He must signify its conclusion to the following Officer, WEST.)

West: Since we are as children, let us sing and dance our way of light around the represented solar point now centred in our circle.

(Here a cheerful circle-chant must accompany the tripping peripheral dance around the flame. Examples of this will be given later. While the circling proceeds, everyone must try his best to visualize, imagine or feel the presence of the inner entity coming to take its place personally in the midst of the dancing invocants. Should the ashes of the petitions be too hot at the end of the dance, the OFFICER OF THE NORTH will take up a small dish of pre-arranged cold ashes, and presenting them to the EAST, say:)

North: I bear the ashes of abandoned hopes.

East: From these, the faithful seed of spirit springs eternally.

(Takes ashes and places them with a pot of earth, knife, or whatever means will be used for planting the selected seed or bulb later.)

South: Thanks be for light arising in the East.
West: May we perceive with it our pathways to perfection.
North: How stand we at this moment?
East: We stand before the light of dawn
That greets a human soul reborn
To mortal life again.
Yet how shall we be truly wise
When new occasions now arise
For pleasure and for pain?
South: Which is the Way to Wisdom?
West: Human trouble mainly springs
From lacking or excess of things
Like two opposing streams.
The art that we should cultivate
Is keeping on a course made straight
Between all such extremes.
North: Blessed be the light that guides our lives, and this, the earth it shines on, that supports our living.

(Here NORTH mixes the ashes with the earth in the pot or pots for seed-planting, then blesses or consecrates the Earth-element according to will, finally presents the earth containers or a single pot to EAST saying:)

As matter has no meaning without mind, so soil has no significance without a seed. Let light breathe forth itself as life.
East: *(Breathes over earth)* By the holy breath in us that is our living spirit, be this substance sanctified for service to our souls.

(Here EAST blesses or consecrates the element of Air as he will.)

South: Good is the ground laid open to the winds of truth and radiated by the sun of righteousness.
West: Life must come from love alone. As water was our one-time womb, and moisture is our mother-milk on earth, let

us approach the spirit set above the waters of compassion and regeneration.

(Here WEST blesses or consecrates the element of Water as he will, but no salt must be put in that portion of the water intended for moistening the seed-pot or pots. Two sorts of cup are useful here, one for the seed, and the other for the people. WEST will deliver the former to the OFFICER OF EAST when it is blessed, and it will be put ready on the altar or whatever surface is otherwise used.)

North: Blessed be the seed implanted in a fertile field, for it will ever grow towards the light with strength and splendour.

East: Blessed be the seed itself, and all that it implies. The very smallest living seed on earth is infinitely greater in its meaning than the mightiest thing mankind will ever make. Consider this tremendous truth with wonder and humility, yet look upon the symbols of its holy mystery with confidence and love, because

> The emblem of a seed
> Shows life divine indeed.

(Here a gong should be sounded, and the meditational emblem of an egg and seeds of some sort set out in a pleasing design is placed where it can conveniently be considered by all, or unveiled if it is there already. Everyone now sits quietly and meditates a few minutes either silently or to suitable music. When this is completed, SOUTH gives the signal to rise, saying:)

South: It is written truthfully that as we sow, we shall eventually reap. Now is the season for our sowing. What seed of light is this which we will plant among us?

West: Let it be duly named and planted deep within us, so that it will germinate and grow into the flower and fruit of all the faith we here and now place in it.

North: May it bring us blessings of the spirit, manifested through our souls and substance, as our minds appreciate this action.

East: *(Selects seed)* Blessed be this chosen seed *(...NAME...)* that comes to life among us here and now. May it open unto us the inner ways we search for and fulfil our present

34

prayers and purpose with its fruits. Be it born of us and bear within it the intentions of our truest will, that it and we may grow together into the eternal Light which emanates and ends each living entity.

(The Name of the seed is the key-word for the Season. As the year progresses it is changed to suit each phase of the solar cycle accordingly.)

(Dipping seed in water:)
O greatest Ocean-Mother of all life,
Unfathomed secret sea.
Bless Thou for us this living link
With Thine infinity.

(As seed emerges from water:)
Welcome to our world, O ...... Blessed be that which comes among us, in the name of the wisdom, the love, the justice, and the infinite mercy of the one eternal spirit, AMEN. *(The Cross is made with these words.)*

ALL: SO MOTE IT BE, AMEN.

South: A seed unplanted is a word unuttered and a power unproven.

West: Blessed be the word that waits within a willing womb.

(Here NORTH kneels towards EAST, holding up cupped hands awaiting the pot of earth.)

North: May emptiness be filled, silence hear the word, stillness move, and darkness be enlightened.

East: *(Places earth-pot in NORTH's hands, makes hole in earth with dagger point or finger, inserts seed, pours in a little water, then smooths earth over, marking the Circle-Cross sign on top.)*
In perfect love,
LET THERE BE LIFE

(Gong. NORTH stands and elevates pot.)

Behold the miracle of life made manifest among us by the law of light; in perfect love BE WHAT THOU WILT.

ALL: O perfect love, BE WHAT THOU WILT.

South: Blessed be this clay and our devoted deed.

West: Blessed be this Springtime and our new-sown seed.

North: Glory be unto the Greatest One to Whom we grow, Whose garden has no limits, and Whose everlasting season never ends.

(If any other pots are to be planted for a special reason, such as other individuals or groups, EAST does this now, simply repeating a brief blessing over each.)

East: *(Invokes:)* O Thou supreme Life-Spirit, cause of every change throughout creation, origin of all, and single source of every living soul, of Thee alone is our beginning, and in Thee alone we have no ending. Blessed be Thy name and names to us for evermore.

As we have duly sown Thy sacred symbol of the seed this Springtime, set Thou likewise in our hearts and souls the sacred spark of Thine immortal light.

Grant us, we pray, a peaceful season of progression. Let us perceive fresh light upon our paths and follow this with faith throughout Thy plans for our perfection. May this truly be Thy will in us and our true will in Thee that we may ultimately unify in everlasting love.

ALL: SO MOTE IT BE, AMEN.

South: Since we have been brought to light and life, be this our cause for celebration with the cup.

West: As Springtime before Summer, work before reward, and innocence before experience, so should water precede wine. It is right and proper that we should partake of water at this season since without it how could wine exist? With pure water be our primal ancestors remembered, for it was the only wine available to them. Because they were, we are together at this time and place. We live from them, their spirits live in us. Blessed be life for evermore.

North: Whoso refuses water rejects life itself. Be it thankfully accepted by us all.

East: Be not bread forgotten so that our descendants may remember us.

South: And may it become for us a staff of life on earth that raises us to perfect light in heaven.

West: Better is the simplest sustenance with love and trust than sumptuous fare with hatred and suspicion.

North: Let us share with one another willingly the least we hold, which may be more than we shall ever have.

(Here the EAST, as principal OFFICER OF THE SEASON, blesses or consecrates the cup of water and platter of bread as he will. These elements may be carried round the circle to each companion by the OFFICER OF THE CORD, or else passed from one to another deosil. When the cup and platter are empty, and recovered by WEST and NORTH respectively, EAST says:)

East: Companions of the year ahead, be cheerful. The seed is sown, the gates are open, and events await us on the way that we must go. Let us sing and dance the season in.

(Here there is music, and a singing dance if space allows. A good action song is very worthwhile, and a splendid one is Green Grow the Rushes O, but with this slightly different sequence:)

One is One and all alone, etc.,
Two, two, the lillywhite boys, etc.,
Three, three, the rivals, etc.,
Four for the heavenly Quarters, etc.,
Five for the symbols at your door, etc.,
Six for the six proud walkers, etc.,
Seven for the seven stars in the sky,etc.,
Eight for the April rainers, etc.,
Nine for the nine bright shiners, etc.,
Ten for the emanations, etc.,
Eleven, the One that went before, etc.,
Twelve for the signs of heaven, etc.

(At conclusion, SOUTH calls to order.)

South: Companions, come to order cheerfully, for all good times must gracefully become a blessed memory. Happily we met, happily we worked, now happily our ways must part that we may meet in happiness again.

West: In what way shall we meet next time?

North: The way for which our word was chosen.
East: What is our password of the period?
ALL: ......
East *(cont.):* Thanks be to the protecting powers that we have
worked these rites in peace, and may we face our future
both with confidence and competence. Be a final blessing
bidden on us, in the name of the wisdom,

and of the love,
and of the justice,
and the infinite mercy
of the One Eternal Spirit,
AMEN.

Now let us close according to established custom.

*(Here the ceremony is rounded off in whatever way is willed by those
that have worked it.)*

The Rite of Summer

✝

The Rite of Summer

*There is maximum light, everyone is alert and in a state of free
motion, miming some task connected with the season. The OFFICER
OF THE SOUTH is Principal. When the moment seems right,
SOUTH sounds a horn, or raps with a staff to call order. All attend.*

South: Companions, let us pause a while to rest from all our
labours in the light, and celebrate our coming season at
this summit of the solar cycle.

West: Blessed be the sun that shines at noon upon our inner day
and throws no shadow on our paths ahead.

North: Blessed be this time of our enlightenment, and welcome
is the warmth with which we ought to live with one
another in this world.

East: Blessed be the light, the love, the learning and the life
whereby we come together for this work.

South: High is Summer. Let our spirits likewise raise themselves
above all clouds of ignorance, so that we may once more
regain the heaven of the splendid stars from whence we
came to earth as solar seeds.

Work with will and play with purest pleasure, o ye
men and maidens of these Mysteries. We have work
to do together with our fellow mortals in the fields of
consciousness which we must cultivate and care for
while we are in human form. There is enjoyment to be
found in every kind of effort when we learn to look for
it with opened inner eyes. However much we may have
done already, there is yet far more for us to bring to light
within this company, and for the good of all with whom
we are concerned.

We need have no fears of failure while the Inner Ones
are with us. Are we not employed upon the greatest work
of all? Surely we are young and strong enough to forge

ahead with perfect faith and confidence that we shall reach the spiritual states we seek if we continue in our cosmic course? However we may lose our way or falter for a moment, can we not recover balance and proceed again whenever we sincerely ask the Holy Ones for Their assistance? Let us call upon Them now, and give the ancient greeting from a mortal striving soul to the Immortal Living Spirit.

I   A   O

(EE)   (YAY)   (YO)

(ALL repeat this sonic resonantly and loudly.)

West: Companions, let us gladly take responsibility for what we are, and all that we may do together. We are no longer helpless children in the Mysteries, but old enough to realize and follow out the meanings of man's oldest faith. The sacred seed we sowed at Springtime has become a precious plant in flower among us. Now it must be cherished carefully, so that its fruit will be our means of life when we have grown beyond these mortal bodies.

Nature flourishes around us, and so we should flourish also. Since our Great Mother shows her beauty, let these members of her family be beautiful likewise. Put out the pleasant signs of Summer with rejoicing and appreciation. Great indeed are They we honour with this happy custom. May They truly link with us through all that lives, and may we learn to link with Them by every leaf upon the tree of life itself.

(Here the signs, garlands, gauds, etc. are set up or distributed. The veiled solar symbol of a flowering yellow plant and appropriate trimmings is either placed ready, or as suitable for production at the meditation period. Music and full movements. When all is ready, NORTH calls to order.)

North: Blessed are the signs of Summer all around us.

East: May they show us how to reach the realms of everlasting youth we hope to find within our hearts held high to Heaven.

South: Let us think about ourselves a while, and wonder what we are accomplishing as willers of the work we claim to care for in the spiritual spheres we are supposed to cultivate. What have we done since Spring to earn our living in the state of light, or claim companionship with Cosmos? Are we worthy or unworthy workers? Who can answer us, excepting Those whose work is done by using us as instruments, and They speak silently. If They spoke with human words, and asked us now what we are doing in their names, how should we answer Them?

West: With faith in confidence.

ALL: With faith in confidence.

North: This is the true tongue of the Holy Ones. If we communicate with Them by our beliefs, They will reply in language that enlightened souls may understand. Let Their aid be asked upon our present undertakings.

East: O Thou Single Source of Light and Life whose scattered seeds we are on earth, thanks be that we have grown and flourished as we stand within Thy garden. Prosper Thou, we pray, whatever further efforts we must make in Thy divine direction.

South: We expect so much from Inner Ones, and now They only ask in gentle ways what we have done on Their behalf, or would accomplish if we could. How have we worked since seed-time? What are we doing now? What are our hopes of harvest? Who is ready with a reasonable answer?

(Here the OFFICER OF THE WEST collects the written petitions and hands them to SOUTH.)

West: On behalf of our companionship, both present and by proxy, I present before these portals the petitions from the hearts and souls of all among us who believe in the essential goodness of the Great Eternal Ones behind our being.

North: Blessed be Their steadfast light beyond all darkness. Now does night pay homage unto everlasting day.

East: Let these emblems of our secret thoughts and prayers be sent through fire to highest light. May reflection upon what has passed illuminate our present, that our future may be clearer to us.

South: *(Stacks petitions in brazier or as for burning)* Blessed be the faithful fires of Summer kindled on the hilltops of the outer world and deep within our hearts in honour of the High Ones we would work for and enjoy existing with. During ages past, we offered blood upon our altars, then progressed to sacrificing fruits of earth or precious gifts. Now we have learned to dedicate our living souls to light, instead of mere material possessions. Here we stand stone-fast within our cosmic circle, offering ourselves as all oblation. May we be accepted in the Spirit moving us to make this true AT-ONE-MENT. May the Blessed ones enlighten us this Summer season, and throughout our time for evermore.

(Here SOUTH consecrates and lights the fire according to will.)

West: Blessed be the sun that comes among us as a friendly fire.

North: Let us dance the measure of this Mystery around and through the flame of faith that we have kindled in the name of light within our circle.

East: And may our spiritual links with inner life become true partners of our progress.

(Here the circle-dance is performed, while the human participants endeavour to 'dance down' the invisible companions among them. They try to dance through the fire in some way, even if a hand is only rapidly passed across the flame. At the conclusion, order is called by SOUTH.)

South: Thanks be for light increased among us.

West: Shining at the sun of Summer overhead.

North: Overcoming all deceits of darkness.

East: How stand we at this moment?

South: We stand between the day and night
When darkness has been lost in light,
Being neither curst nor blest.
Betwixt this way of wrong and right,
Our choice is clear through black and white.
The middle path is best.

ALL: Show us the way and we will follow.

West: The way is straight, the path is long,
While flesh is weak, but spirit strong,
We need to BE, and KNOW.

Who enters life is past recall,
For none may rise save we that fall,
ABOVE is reached BELOW.

North: How blows the wind of Summer?

East: It blows our blossoms into their full flowering. Blessed be the light revealing their true beauty to beholders by the inner sight. Blessed also be the wholesome air that brings us inspiration as we breathe it with belief.

(Here OFFICER OF THE EAST blesses and consecrates the element of Air according to will. Flower petals may be scattered during this.)

South: A miracle has come among us as an answer to our prayers. Here is a work of wonder wrought by the Creative Ones themselves, and utterly beyond our human hands to make, or mortal minds' design.

    Behold might manifest as mercy in the lovely form of flowers. Contemplate the blessing of such beauty both with reverence and rapture. None but divinity itself would dare conceive simplicity in such a supreme way as this.

(Here the floral emblem is produced and contemplated in silence or to suitable music. At the conclusion WEST speaks:)

West: From what seed sprang this bloom before us?

North: From ... that was sown last Spring.

East: How shall we name the flower among us?

South: Let us agree to call it ......

ALL: SO MOTE IT BE, AMEN.

South *(cont.)*: Blessed be this flower that has been brought to bloom within our Cosmic Circle as a symbol of the spirit in whose beauty we believe with our whole hearts. May we flourish faithfully, and grow to grace the gardens of eternal glory, in the name of the wisdom,
>>> and of the love,
>>> and of the justice,
>>> and the infinite mercy,
>>> of the One Eternal Spirit,
>>> AMEN.

ALL: SO MOTE IT BE, AMEN.

West: Whoso plucks a flower prevents a fruit.

North: Let us continue with its cultivation, that the fruit may form.

East: Be it so with water and with willing work.

South: May the waters of the west work well with us.

West: *(Here blesses or consecrates the element of Water in a ewer, basin or pool, as the case may be, concluding:)*

Only over water may the greatest name of all be uttered. Though no mortal mouth may give this forth, we offer up our call above the water to the winds of Heaven hoping that we may be heard by That which brought us into being.

I   A   O

(EE)   (YAH)   (YOH)

(The call is sounded over the water to the Four Quarters by WEST, but if that Officer cannot do this properly, any of the companions may give it, or all may do it together.)

North: Let an echo of this universal utterance reach everyone within our world.

East: May it be borne by every breath of air.

South: May it be flashed by every form of fire.

West: May it be written with each wave of water.

North: May the word of will in us be felt as firmly as this earth beneath our feet.

(Here the OFFICER OF NORTH consecrates the element of Earth according to will; at the conclusion OFFICER OF EAST says:)

East: How shall our purely human hands not tire of everlasting toil with this, or any other sort of earth?

South: By refreshing them with radiance from our immortal sun of spirit, and by plunging them within the pool of peace profound.

West: Come then, companions, wash away with will our weariness from work or worry in this world. Be rested and regenerated by the waters of compassion, in the depths of which the supreme spirit of surpassing love renews the life of every single soul.

(Here the whole company of the circle ablute. They may file around the circle past the WEST point, dipping their fingers and drying them, or the water may be borne around the circle by the OFFICER OF THE CORD, or they may work as they will, but as each one ablutes, the WEST says:)

West *(cont.)*: Be purity and peace upon you, in the name, etc.

(At conclusion, NORTH says:)

North: As water opens up the way for wine, now let perfume mark our pathways to perfection.

East: What must we give to gain perfection?

South: A flower gives out its perfume to the atmosphere of all the world, and yet retains its own perfection for itself. So does the goodness of the Great Ones come to all of us without diminishing the single source of its supply.

As our animals communicate by means of scent, and flowers by fragrance, so has the human soul an odour of its own, pervading worlds most proper to itself.

Therefore we should learn to live so that we may make a pleasant perfume for the Inner Ones as we approach Them. To this end let us anoint ourselves in honour of the Blessed Ones whose company we seek this season and for evermore.

(Blesses anointing oil, saying:)

Blessed be the fragrance of this oil wherewith both light and beauty may be manifest about us. By sharing its aroma, may we truly be of one accord as a most welcome savour to the High Ones unto whom we now aspire in spirit. May it help to cover our remaining human imperfections with its perfume as we present ourselves before the Holy Presence, in the name, etc.

Come then, companions, let us be anointed with the sacred scent by which true dedicants to light and beauty are made known to one another, and the single spirit that all serve together. May the fragrance of the simplest flower provide us with sufficient faith to lead us into PEACE PROFOUND for evermore.

(Here the companions either file past the OFFICER OF THE SOUTH, who anoints them, or he goes around the circle, depending on convenience. As he anoints each, he says:)

May light and beauty be upon you in the name of
>The wisdom *(forehead)*
>The love *(chin)*
>The justice *(right cheek)*
>and the infinite mercy *(left cheek)*
>of the One Eternal Spirit *(encircle face)*
>AMEN *(under nose)*.

(SOUTH anoints himself last. At conclusion, WEST says:)

West: Let the cup be circulated, that we may be cheered upon our ways of light. Of olden times our ancestors used ale to celebrate this season, since it seemed to them the blood of that beneficence which brought them barley bread. Let us share this symbol gladly in our company with that same spirit which commenced the custom and continues it among us at the present time.

North: As ale is liquid, bread is solid grain. Let the cakes of bread be not forgotten. They make good bodies for a willing soul to live in.

East: Be a blessing bidden upon both.

(Here the OFFICER OF THE SOUTH, as principal, blesses the cup, which may have barley wine in it if ale is not wanted, and also the bread-cakes. These are passed round the circle first, and the cup last. At conclusion, SOUTH says:)

South: Blessed be this season of the Summer sun, and all it shines on visibly or inwardly. Even though it may be hidden from us by the darkest clouds, let us ever keep its glorious light undimmed within us, shining in our hearts and radiating warmth around us unto every other soul.

West: Be the season started with a cheerful song. Let us make melody among us.

(Here is the song of the season according to choice. At its conclusion, NORTH calls to order.)

North: Companions, come to order cheerfully, for all good things must sometime be a blessed memory. Happy did we meet, now happy let us part, that happily we all may meet again together.

East: In what way shall we meet again?

South: The way for which our word was chosen. What is that word?

ALL: ...... *(repeat password.)*

South *(cont.):* In that way of light let us proceed in peace with thanks to the Eternal Ones that we have worked our rite according to our will. Now let us close in our accustomed manner. In the name, etc.

(Here the procedure of closing takes place as the companions will.)

A suggestion for a midsummer song in traditional form is as follows:

1 Now is high midsummer sun,
    hay down, hi down, ho down, hu-u down.
  But living time is never done,
    hay down, ho down, deri down day.
2 Cease all sorrow, stop all strife, etc.,
  Come hopeful hearts and a happy life, etc.
3 If you mind midsummer day, etc.,
  Luck and love will come your way, etc.
4 Joy and gladness, good and true, etc.,
  Come to me and go to you, etc.
5 Who is older than the sun? etc.,
  That in whom all lives are one, etc.
6 Who is wiser than the rest? etc.,
  Only who knows what is best, etc.
7 Who is greatest of the great? etc.,
  That which stays the hand of fate, etc.
8 Who is higher than the sky? etc.,
  Whoso outgrows the tallest lie, etc.
9 If you would have every right, etc.,
  Follow on the way of light, etc.
10 Here is common sense to try, etc.,
  Do as you would be done by, etc.

11 Here is counsel to fulfil, etc.,
      If you harm none do what you will, etc.
12 Now be gladsome, light and gay, etc.,
      On this good midsummer day, etc.

This makes a good on-the-spot sort of dance, if at the first 'Hay, down, ho down' line a rotation on axis and a stamp to each Quarter is made, and on the second 'Deri down day' line, a complete spin is made.

✝

The Rite of Autumn

✝
The Rite of Autumn

The place is lit as for sunset. Harvest signs evident. The principal Officer is WEST. Everyone has taken on an air of being middle-aged and prosperous, cheerful to a degree and relaxed in character. When the time seems ripe, WEST calls to order by sharpening steel on stone briskly and saying:

West: Companions, here at last comes harvest time that we have worked for. Blessed be the fruits of our endeavours and the generosity of the Immortal Ones that gave us grace to gather them.

North: Let all be safely stored against the waiting days of Winter when the longest shadows lie across the land.

East: As carefully collected provender protects us from the full effects of famine upon earth, so may the contents of our minds and souls provide against our spiritual starvation.

South: Hearty be our harvest, and in highest honour held the willing hands that bring it home for us.

West: Nothing is for nothing in all worlds. As we sowed and tended, so must we now reap. At this season of requital and reward we have to ask the Great Ones for our due returns from service in their fields. We shall be fairly and most fully paid for what we have accomplished, and even granted credit for our good intentions. Nothing will be held from us that we deserve, nor can we possibly be cheated by, or cheat ourselves, the All-aware Accountant of our actions. Let us call attention from the Inner Beings of our beliefs by uttering the ancient cry,

I   A   O

(EE)   (YAY)   (YOH)

ALL: *(Echo call vibrantly.)*

North: May we ourselves become the welcome harvest of the Blessed Ones upon this earth.

East: Companions, what sort of harvest have we any right to hope for in exchange for our endeavours of the past? If we claim rewards for what we did that was worthwhile, we must risk retribution for our less deserving deeds. Who is sure enough of how they stand in spiritual status to make definite demands for what divinity may owe them?

Now that night and day are equal, we have this brief opportunity for balancing the best against the worst in us, and asking the Eternal Ones to compensate the difference as lightly as may be.

Let us set out the signs and symbols of this Autumn season, so that we may honour with due forms the spiritual power providing what is due to us.

(Here the signs, garlands, etc. are set out according to will. Most importantly needed is the emblem of meditation, which must include stems of ripe wheat or barley. There should be a dish of assorted fruits, at least one fruit per person. A small sickle or shears of the ritual type should be available. Music of an autumnal sort. When all is ready, SOUTH speaks:)

South: Blessed be the hearty signs of Autumn gathered pleasantly around us.

West: Companions, let us try and realize what we are worth intrinsically as individual living souls. We obviously cannot know our value to the Highest One, nor should we ever set too low an estimate on our most irreplaceable and precious legacy of light.

How can we honestly put prices on ourselves, and say sincerely what we should receive as due returns for what we think we have accomplished on behalf of those from whom we claim our recompense? We are worth no more nor less to the Eternal Ones than They are worth to us as spiritual standards which we value as the fundamental basis of our beings, behaviour and beliefs. Who dares declare what this may be in each of us?

Yet our time has come within this solar cycle when we have the right and privilege to ask the Holy Ones for our fair share of what we are entitled to, by what we have become within ourselves since we began to earn our self-existence. If They asked us in return what we consider our true compensation ought to he, how should we answer Them?

North: In absolute sincerity, not fearing the Requiting Ones nor favouring ourselves.

East: As we deal with Them, so may They duly deal with us.

South: Be a blessing bidden upon us and on our harvest work that waits our hands.

West: O Thou Perfect Power of Providence, from whom proceeds all we shall ever be, bless thou what we may gather of thy bounty and beneficence from every source supplying our spiritual needs. Let the level of our measure be according to the balance of thy might and mercy. In the name, etc.

North: Naught pays for naught on inner, as on outer, levels of our lives. If we set no value on ourselves, then how may we expect the Holy Ones to value us? Let us at least present our personal petitions to those Mighty Beings. They will deal with us according to the way we deal with them in honesty and honour.

East: May our offerings from earth be found of good account by Heaven.

(Here the SOUTH collects accounts, or the OFFICER OF THE CORD may do so, and these are presented to the West Portal.)

South: On behalf of our companionship, both present and by proxy, I present these true petitions of our hopes this harvest time among us all who work with will in spiritual fields of inner cultivation.

West: May these be accepted in the spirit they are offered, and according to the asking may the answers be received in recompense for what has been requested. Let us submit these estimations of ourselves to the decisive test of fire, from whence the burning light of truth alone emerges. This should be sufficient for each honest soul to recognize his proper payment.

North: Blessed be the careful fire of Autumn, ripening the fruits of earth, and separating good from worthless growth.

East: May what we sow on earth be reaped by Heaven, and the seeds which we have sown in spirit come to wholesome harvest in this world.

South: O Thou Eternal One from Whom our lives originate, and by Whose grace we grow to what is best we should become, take Thou our thoughts and turn them into things, as we take things and turn them into thoughts.

Here are the tokens of our self-esteem on earth. We only offer them as a sincere attempt to bring ourselves before thee for whatever we are worth as souls who seek to serve Thy cause of Cosmos. Measure these against Thy boundless love in which we trust completely, then – be it AS THOU WILT with us forever.

May the light of sunset shine resplendently on us this Autumn equinox, that the surpassing glory of the heavens might enfold us for a single moment here and now on earth.

(Here the petitions are stacked, the fire lit and consecrated by SOUTH.)

West: Blessed be the sun of Autumn bringing heavenly beauty to the edges of this earth.

North: Let that same sun be danced among us down into our circle.

East: That we may receive our due rewards with gladness and rejoicing.

(Here the circle-dance is done to appropriate seasonal chanting. At conclusion, SOUTH says:)

South: Glory be unto the golden light by which we shall ourselves be glorified.·

West: Thanks be for light descending to this level of our lives.

North: That we may be illuminated by its richest rays.

East: Blessed be light so wonderfully shown to us upon its path of power.

South: How stand we on that path this moment?

West: We stand between the light and shade
Upon the middle path we made
Where day and night divide,
As we have lived and worked and prayed,
We now expect to be repaid
With neither shame nor pride.

ALL: How shall we find our true fulfilment?

North: Fire and water bring to birth
With air, the outcome of this earth.
For this we know without a doubt,
Our seed goes in, and fruits come out.
So bless the earth on which we stand
For harvests of the sea and land.

East: How fare the fields of Autumn?

South: Roots below, fruits above, ripe and ready for our reaping.

West: Blessed be the earth supporting life, and air that brings the breath of life to earth. Let us keep our feet well grounded on our earth however high we hold our heads to Heaven. So shall we live as upright souls between both ends of our existence.

North: In ancient times, mankind approached the earth as our own mother, from whose womb we came to incarnation, by whose breasts we lived, and whose loving mouth devoured us at our deaths. Why should we deny the basics of this beautiful belief, by which we once enjoyed the closest possible relationship between ourselves and the creative spirit that conceived us? Blessed be our Mother Earth indeed, and every single soul evolving with her.

(Here the NORTH blesses or consecrates the element of earth according to will. At the conclusion, EAST takes up the tale:)

East: Likewise did our forebears see the sunlit sky as father-fount of all fertility. It arched above our Mother Earth, and showered down seeds of living souls like scattered raindrops on the surface of the world. Who shall say with certainty from what strange star our souls originated and arrived upon this planet to possess and animate these forms of flesh which breathe the atmosphere of earth? Who sees where we will go when all the air around us is unfit for human use? Blessed indeed be our true source of spiritual inspiration, and the father-force creating our immortal spirits from the living light.

(Here the EAST consecrates and blesses the element of Air according to will. At conclusion, SOUTH says:)

South: What is the most we may expect on earth?

West: Our highest hope of harvest is to grow beyond necessity of being embodied, and exist in fuller freedom by the means of finer forces than are practical to us at present. Since we are not ready for such reaping, here is our symbolic substitute in shape of fruitful forms which none but nature may mature for our consumption, that we may continue on our cosmic course. Let us be conscious of its inner content.

(Here the meditation symbol is produced. It has stems of ripe corn at the centre, and assorted fruits or vegetables round the edges. Music as suitable. When period of contemplation is complete, NORTH says:)

North: How did all these fruits develop?
East: They matured from ...... that flowered in Summer.
South: What shall we name it now?
West: Be it named among us ......
ALL: SO MOTE IT BE, AMEN.
West *(cont.):* Blessed be our harvest fairly earned by all the efforts we have made to grow more perfectly toward our light this solar cycle. May it be sufficient to sustain our souls throughout the coming seasons. Let us remember it by name as ...... In the name, etc.
North: Whoso eats a fruit will surely sacrifice its seed.
East: Who eats not lives not. Sacrifice selects the seed that should survive to spread its species in their finest forms.
South: May we ourselves be chosen to continue as evolving entities when the instant of divine decision is upon us.
West: Whatever comes to us of any lasting value should be well and truly earned by our own efforts to become the sort of spiritual beings our true wills realize we ought to be. Such a heavenly harvest lies within our hands on earth, so here and now let willing hands be dedicated to this duty.

(Spitting on right hand:)
BLESSED BE THE HAND PUT FORTH WITH MIGHT.
(ALL repeat.)

(Spitting on left hand:)
BLESSED BE THE HAND PUT FORTH WITH MEANING.
(ALL repeat.)

(Rubbing both hands vigorously:)
BLESSED BE WHAT WE MUST DO WITH MIGHT
AND MEANING, THAT OUR HANDS MAY HOLD
THE HARVEST OF OUR HIGHEST HOPES.
(ALL repeat.)

West *(cont.):* Companions, out of all that we have been, a seed
must be selected out of which will grow the souls and
selves we shall become. This is a constant process, and the
favoured moment for our choice is always NOW.

Every instant brings our re-becoming in some way. We
die and are reborn with every breath. Let us only save the
very best in us for seeds to plant more perfectly at every
step we take upon the spiral of the solar seasons leading
upwards to the Ultimate of Highest Light. With all the
will which we may bring to bear on this most special
stroke of our selective sickle, let us now in Sacred Silence,

CHOOSE. CUT. CHERISH.

*(Here OFFICER OF WEST raises sickle or shears, and reaps a single
ear of wheat or grain. This is elevated and borne to the altar in
silence. Momentary pause for individual intentions to be made. A
soft clap of hands may terminate this period.)*

North: Blessed be that attaining WHAT IT WILLS TO BE in
peace profound.
East: What shall we attain unless we eat what providence has
ripened for us on the tree of life? In with the harvest!
South: Which way is best for us to gather it?
West: With willing hands, happy hearts and singing souls. Let
the season be sung in.

*(Here the song of the season is sung according to will. At the end,
NORTH says:)*

North: Here is harvest. Be the call of celebration sounded.
East: Loud and clear above the water of the wise.
South: What is the water of the wise?
West: The essence of experience, or juice of judgment, likened
to a fermentation from that fruit which grew upon the
tree of knowledge. This is what we really harvest from

our human lives on earth, and that is why we choose an apple-ale or cider for potation at this solar season. May it indeed sustain us through our times of trial, refresh us when occasions for rejoicing arise, and be as the waters of eternal life, by which we grow to highest light in PEACE PROFOUND. Let our call be clearly heard by all that listen in the compass of complete compassion.

(Here the OFFICER OF THE WEST blesses the cup of cider which is the element of water for this season. The call must be sounded over it to the Four Quarters. I. A. O. is most generally given, but the call may be given by sounding a horn above the cup. At conclusion of this, NORTH says:)

North: Let the cakes of fruit and bread be shared among us who have surely earned them by our efforts. Bread for work, fruit for refreshment, salt for sense, and spice for pleasure. Such are the ingredients of life on earth we mix together. We must combine the right proportions properly, if we would eat enjoyably the bread of our own baking. Blessed may it be for us.

(Here the bread is blessed by WEST and circulated round the companions by the way of light. The cup follows. There may be music during this if time seems to justify it. At conclusion, EAST says:)

East: As we have willed and worked with one another, so may we ever reap the benefits of all we have attempted in our common cause of Cosmos.

South: Are we fully satisfied? Has everyone sufficient for his present needs until we are provided for again?

West: Companions, by the love that binds us in the circle-cross of Cosmos at all solar seasons, let us freely share our spiritual assets with each other, as and when necessity directs. None should lack what love can well afford to give most willingly. If we care nothing for conditions of imbalance and disharmony in this immediate circle of companionship, how shall we dare demand assistance from superior spiritual sources? We only have the right to ask for inner aid when humanly available supplies are insufficient to support our souls. Our petitions otherwise are purely a privilege which we should not presume to demand. Let us therefore help each other very willingly in every way that leads to our eventual enlightenment.

North: No unsought aid must be imposed on any soul. All should be free to ask and answer AS THEY WILL.

East: Blessed be they that set no price upon themselves nor make undue demands for anything they do in spiritual spheres. They shall surely reap the harvest of a heart in harmony with Heaven.

South: May our lengthening shadows in the setting sun become most perfect pointers on our paths ahead, and lead us steadily to hidden light beyond our present horizons.

West: Companions, let us cheerfully complete the purpose of this pleasant circle. Willingly we came together, and with will we worked. Now we must willingly part company, that in goodwill our ways will meet again. What is our word of will for this occasion?

ALL: ......

West (cont.): Thanks be that we have worked our rites in peace. Let us go forth upon our ways according to the will within the word uniting our intentions, and may happy harmony prevail among us from this time as long as light may let it last. Now let us close in our accustomed manner. In the name, etc.

(Here the fruits may be divided among the company, and individual ears of grain reaped if required. There should certainly be some kind of harvest feast afterwards, and suitable singing. A good seasonal action song during which miming is possible, especially in the chorus, is as follows:)

HARVEST SONG

1   The fruits of the earth may be sent from above,
     And we should improve them with wisdom and love.
     If apples and grapes are both products divine,
     Who prefers water to cider or wine?

Chorus (with action)
Up with a ladder and down with the fruits,
In with a shovel and out with the roots.
The Gods may provide us with life from the land,
But the harvest we hold is the work of our hand.

2   Dame Nature's a wonder, we all do agree.
Who knows our necessities better than she?
Yet though she is doing as well as she can,
She answers her best to the touch of a man!
(Chorus)

3   The wheat and the barley as much as the corn
Have kept us alive ever since we were born.
But unless we had turned them to flour and bread,
Few would be living, and many be dead.
(Chorus)

4   We pray for the seasons to be as they should.
Dry or wet weather may do our crops good.
Though if sunshine is needed to ripen the grain,
Who risks rheumatics by working in rain?
(Chorus)

5   Whatever the task, and wherever the field,
We reap our reward with the sickles we wield,
For if all things grew from their numberless seeds,
The whole of our world would be covered in weeds.
(Chorus)

6   So here's to the Gods and the men of this earth
Who take one another for what they are worth.
Each of them doing what has to be done,
In order to live altogether as ONE.
(Chorus)

The Rite of Winter

✝

The Rite of Winter

The place is as dimly lit as possible, while still allowing scripts to be read. All colour is very sober, and everyone is in an elderly and tolerant mood as if at the end of long and well-spent lives. The principal Officer is NORTH. The Companions are seated quietly when NORTH brings them slowly to their feet by four knocks or stamps on the ground.

North: Companions, it is time we rested from our labours for a season, and reposed with nature through the Winter night to come.

East: What shall we do while we are separated from the sun?

South: Recuperate our strength, and rectify our past mistakes as far as we are able. Let us be well rid of all our rubbish in the solstice fire, and sleep a while to find the future in our dreams, then wake and realize them in the world of light.

West: Let us indeed seek slumber with our Mother Nature. She will be kind to us, with her soft songs reminding us of wonders in the past and promises of paradise to come. She alone will try to teach us wisdom while we wait within her womb before we are reborn to active living in the light.

North: Whatever we have been has made us what we are this very moment. All we shall ever be commences at this very moment. Now is always the best moment for reflection on the past in order to project our purpose into future and much finer forms. This is the proper time and season of the solar cycle to be free from whatsoever hinders us from making progress, and for clearing up completely all obscurities which might prevent our passage on the path of light. Such an opportunity should not slip by unnoticed or unused by us.

Let us call upon the Old and Wise Ones in the hope that They will hear and help us.

I   A   O

(EE) (YAY) (YO)

(ALL echo the call with deep resonance.)

East: We are passing rapidly enough towards the closing of our lives for this past solar cycle. When human beings grow old, we tend to think too much about the past because we fear, or cannot find a welcome way to face our future. Surely in this circle our experience of life has led us to expect far more than mere cessation at the ending of our earth-existence? Let us look forward to continuance in Cosmos. Why should we be always bound to mortal bodies, when we might express ourselves as entities in many better ways, away from this one world, in one of all the others there are for us to find? Having done our duty here, we should be glad to go elsewhere in order to enjoy existing otherwise. Meanwhile, we ought to be as happy and harmonious as our humanity occasionally allows on this earth. Let the signs and symbols of the season be set out among us, so that we may celebrate our closure of the solar cycle cheerfully.

(Here the signs and symbols are placed – the traditional evergreens, garlands, etc. The meditation symbol is some kind of a platter with earth on it and dead leaves, twigs and so forth in random patterns. These are set fire to, so ought to be dry. Music as suitable. SOUTH calls to order:)

South: Blessed be these signs of Winter unto us that wait with patience in this world to find our way into another.

West: We should not look back upon the outworn old, except for guidance to the needed new.

North: Companions, we are at the ending of our solar year, and what have we accomplished in that period to bring us spiritual satisfaction with a clear conscience? Are we content with our past service in the cause of Cosmos? How otherwise would we behave, if our last set of seasons lay before, instead of being, as they lie, behind us? This is the final opportunity among ourselves for thinking of these things, and meeting our reflections in the mirror of our memories. Whether we enjoy this self-encounter or endure it, the experience should certainly be undergone by every soul in search of spirit. If the Lords of Life should ask us at this instant what defects of character or imperfections in ourselves we would be free from, if Their will and ours agreed, how should we reply?

East: With true humility and highest hope.

South: As we allow for others' faults, so may allowances be made for ours.

West: Be a blessing bidden on us so that we may pass this Winter season peacefully.

North: O Compassionate and Understanding One, in Whom our endings are but new beginnings of another way of life, be merciful to we who wait before the gates of Winter with anxiety or apprehension. Temper Thou for us the bitter winds and biting frosts we fear to face in spiritual solitude. May the welcome warmth of Thy eternal love envelop and protect us from the perils of this period, comforting our souls and caring for their safety. In the name, etc.

East: None are secure in idleness. Outer rest and inner action serve each other's purpose in the surest way. Let us now consider how we seem as individual souls, and then approach the Mighty Ones with our ideas about improving our integrity by altering our attitudes with Their assistance.

(Here the petitions to that effect are gathered by SOUTH or by OFFICER OF CORD, and presented at NORTH. SOUTH speaks:)

South: On behalf of our companionship, both present and by proxy, I present before these portals our petitions for the faults we find with our own natures to be dealt with by divinity according to the will made one between us.

West: May we never mourn our former failures, but anticipate far more success with our achievements in the future.

North: *(Invokes):* O Ancient and Eternal Spirit unto Whom our entities are simply energies to be emanated into existence AS THOU WILT, Thou alone art PERFECT POWER.

Take Thou our offered imperfections and convert them AS THOU WILT to whatsoever forms of force we might most carefully control upon a cosmic course.

Let not Thy light depart from us forever at this solstice, leaving us to end despairingly in darkness and extinction. Permit us to continue round the circle of creation, and complete what Thou commenced with our original conception in Thy likeness brought to independent life by Thine imaginative will.

(Petitions stacked for burning.)

East: Blessed be the fire of faith that burns on earth this season, shining forth in friendly substitution for the sun.

South: Leave us not, O Light on Whom our spiritual lives depend for their direction.

Take thyself not from us, O Thou Torch of Truth and sole illuminator of our ignorance.

Forsake us not, O Flame of Freedom to proceed the way we will to thy perfection.

Be thou for each and every soul the sacred spark of spirit, round which they revolve unceasingly in their cosmic circles of thy living light.

(Here the SOUTH blesses or consecrates the fire, lights petitions, etc. At conclusion WEST speaks:)

West: Let us enjoy the bright and blessed beauty of a friendly fire.

North: May the faith and friendship that we share in spirit round our fireside never fail this circle of companionship or any other in the world this coming season. However cold and bitter it may be elsewhere, may we always welcome one another in our hearts and homes with warmth enough to overcome the very worst of Winter. Now let us see if we have sufficient strength for our feet to follow the returning solar rays around the symbol by which we represent them.

(Here the circle-dance is performed. This is somewhat slow and steady, in the manner of old people enjoying unusual activity. At the end, EAST speaks:)

East: Thanks be for warmth and close companionship with kindred souls.

South: May we continue so forever in the kindest light.

West: How stand we on its path this moment?

North: We stand in the perplexing night,
With insufficiency of light
To see what lies ahead.
So now with skyward gaze, we plead
All Heaven for one star to lead
The living-and the dead!

ALL: What will happen while our sun is hidden from us?

East: The deepest night no one need dread
Who finds safe guiding light ahead.
Within us glows a sacred spark
Which we should follow through the dark
With perfect faith its star-like ray
Will lead us to a better day.

South: How is it with the earth in Winter?

West: Bleak and barren above, rich and resting below. Hands find what eyes see not.

North: Blessed be the earth at rest beneath our feet, as we have hope of rest in peace one day with earth above our heads. Be it remembered peace is not a static state, but is the perfect poise of power. Not cessation, but completion and continuation. May there be peace on earth to all mankind that bear goodwill to one another.

(Here NORTH blesses or consecrates the element of Earth, while companions tread the ground as if warming feet on an icy day. At conclusion, the meditational emblem is produced and displayed. It is simply a small heap of dead combustible twigs and leaves. NORTH continues:)

North: Behold what dead disorders and what muddled minds we may encounter if we live in human bodies long enough to meet them. How sad it is that we might come to such confusion of our consciousness if we outstay our welcome in this world. Surely it is best for outworn beings and bodies to return to earth for their renewal rather than remain imprisoned uselessly by human incarnation.

Nature never wastes such opportunities in her economy, for she changes chaos into Cosmos by the redistribution of disintegrating force-forms. We can work this alchemy of alteration for ourselves if we so will. Let us attempt to learn whatever lesson contemplation may communicate to us on this occasion.

(Here the symbol is contemplated either silently or to suitable music. At the end, EAST says:)

East: Where did all this debris fall from?
South: From ...... of the Autumn.
West: What shall we name it now?
North: Be it known to us henceforth as ......
ALL: SO MOTE IT BE, AMEN.
North *(cont.)*: Blessed be the end of our endeavours on this earth for the past solar cycle. May we face our future through the season set before us, with calm confidence that we are following with fearless faith the cosmic course that we have chosen to call ......   In the name, etc.
East: What shall we do with all the residue remaining with us here and now?
South: Let us burn it into beauty that it may become a beacon of deliverance from darkness, and finally a fertilizing ash to aid arising growth in future fields.
ALL: SO MOTE IT BE.
South *(cont.)*: *(Lights pyre)* By the light of the past be the future perceived.
West: By what we have learned be new teaching received.
North: By that which is left, may we find what is right.
East: By the fire that is spent, may we come to fresh light.
South: What is keener than the worst of Winter winds?
West: The bitter blow to self-esteem exposing all the difference between the sort of soul we ought to be, and those we are as actualities.
North: Surely we should equalize these two extremities, and look between them both to recognize a middle path of poise that leads to light above the pillars of opposed opinions. So may we reach a reasonable measure of respect for what we surely will be, if we seek real inspiration from our inner sources of intelligence and spiritual strength.

East: *(Invokes:)* O Infinite Intelligence in Whom all inspiration is, tell us the truth about ourselves in whatsoever ways we best may bear without being broken by that burden. Deal lightly with us, O Divine Directing One, that we may learn our lessons of this life through love, yet with an unassuming air of absolute and utter confidence in Thy complete command of Cosmos.

(Here the OFFICER OF EAST blesses or consecrates element of Air. After that, SOUTH says:)

South: There is no best or worst to find or fear within us saving that which we have made ourselves.

West: Even as most welcome water is withheld from eager earth by freezing up its flow with chilling cold, so does spiritual bitterness inhibit our most needed waters of compassion, isolating souls in icy solitude by lack of love. Let us not allow such coldness in our circle that might cause our cup to freeze and fail its function of supplying the free and friendly spirit we should seek to share among us. As ordinary ice will melt within a cup held closely to our hearts, so may the slightest chill within our souls be banished by the spirit of surpassing love itself, through all the willing warmth we ought to hold towards each other from our truest heart of hearts.

(Here the OFFICER OF WEST blesses or consecrates the element of Water in the form of ice, suitably contrived either in a cup not needed later, or in the same cup which will presently be used for iced spirits or other chilled drink, depending on which symbol is willed. At conclusion of this, NORTH invites:)

North: Come then, O companions, that each soul of us may find what he amounts to as an individual, by looking for his image in the magic mirror which reflects reality according to the light emitted by that soul itself. A taper, to be lit by everyone, is representative of revelation which has been or is to be received. As we look our last upon the fading face of the past period, let us see ourselves reflected from it, and consider how we might improve that image in the season set before us with this opportunity.

(Here the companions file past the NORTH point. First a dark reflector is presented before their faces, then a white one, after which they are given a taper or candle, which they must light from the NORTH flame, before they continue circling back to their places. The words said by NORTH during this action are:)

North *(cont.)*: *(Black reflector)* Behold the one you were.
(White reflector) Behold the one you might be.
(Lighted flame) Behold the one you are to light.

(When this circling is concluded, EAST says:)

East: May our true reflections be revealed to us most brightly by the welcome wine of wisdom.

South: Let the cup of our companionship be circulated in the way of light around our circle.

West: From hand to hand, mouth to mouth, mind to mind, and heart to heart among us all.

North: Be this season celebrated with the symbol of good wine, like that of life itself, pressed from us by experience at first, and then maturing as we mellow with it, to become much better beings than we were at birth. Nothing else than ageing rightly makes a wine worth while, nor will the savour of our souls seem right for this till we are old enough and able to appreciate the taste of truth.

East: May this never be too strong for us to bear with benefit, but only serve to stimulate our search for spirit.

South: Consider well the rich rewarding cakes with which this solstice is remembered. They represent the only realistic wealth within us, which belongs of right unto our souls alone, all else being left behind us with our bodies. These cakes remind us that our finest qualities in life are left until the last on earth, when what is best in us begins to live in Heaven. May all that we remember of our earth lives afterwards be as sweet and satisfying as the richness of these symbols.

West: Be a blessing bidden on them both.

North: Blessed be the forms of flesh and blood which we must share together, since we are but individual atoms of the body which belongs to universal spirit. This is the mystery of light made manifest as living man. Whether in or out of human incarnation, may each single soul be guided to its proper place within the perfect plan, and live in ultimate enlightenment with PEACE PROFOUND.

(Here the wine and cakes are blessed or consecrated by NORTH and distributed around the circle. At the end, EAST says:)

East: May we truly pass beyond our bodies by the blessed bridge that leads to perfect peace in living light.

South: Let us sing the passing season of our lives to sleep.

(Here the slumber-song is sung. The tone of the rite becomes very quiet and hushed from this point on, the few remaining lines being taken somewhat sotto voce, as if for fear of waking someone. When song is sung, WEST says gently:)

West: With whom lies the last word?

North: With that by whom the first was uttered. In the beginning was the word of power. At the ending comes the word of peace. With that word let us pass according to the WILL WITHIN. What is our present word?

ALL: ......

North *(cont.)*: Peacefully we met, and peacefully we worked, now let us part in peace, that we may meet once more that blessed way. Closed be this rite according to our custom. In the name, etc.

SLEEPING SONG

1   The last year of life has gone past our recalling,
Except for our feelings of pride or regret.
Of all that was dreadful, just dull, or enthralling,
What should we remember, and how much forget?

> *Chorus*
> Sleep! Deep! Hoping to wake with the Blest.
> Dream! Scheme! How we may live for the best.
> Our past left behind leaves a future to find,
> So now let us thankfully rest.

2   Is a Beneficent Being above us?
Or nothing whatever concerned with our fate.
Are there good spirits that care for and love us?
Or none but ourselves to consider our state.

(Chorus)

3   What is the meaning of human existence?
And may we become any more than mere man?
Such vital enigmas demand with insistence,
We seek their solutions however we can.

(Chorus)

4   If reincarnation should ever restore us
To birth beyond reach of a blessing or curse,
And we had our lives once again set before us,
Should we do better, or might we be worse?

(Chorus)

5   Blessed be life beyond all need of dying,
And happy the soul with no burden to shed,
Yet who knows, without any thought of denying,
Whether it's best to be living or dead?

(Chorus)

6   Our questions are answered by living and learning
Whatever comes next on the path we must plod,
Between birth and death while we have means of earning,
The wisdom that makes man become like a God.

(Chorus)

✝

The Sense of the Ceremonies

✝

The Sense of the Ceremonies

S UCH are the Rites of the Seasons in accordance with ancient tradition, but brought up to date in method and manner of expression. If carried out with regularity for several years, they will achieve a state of spiritual solidarity among practitioners which leads to very deep levels of inner life indeed. Eventually, they will become the turning points around which the cosmic life and consciousness of the circle-companions revolve; they will become the central nucleus of divine light. This makes an incredible difference to all concerned. Instead of their lives being merely affairs of casual consciousness tied up with the ephemera of mundane existence, they will discover, as a basis for their being, really solid spiritual ground whose existence is eternal and immortal.

We are and shall become according to our own basic beliefs, motivations, behaviour, and the course of our consciousness. If these are no more than purely materialistic, permitting us no further life than that confined to earthly events, how much greater can we possibly grow? On the other hand, if we devalue our humanity to a point where we are content to drift around in an aimless, cloud-cuckoo-land of muddled mysticism, we shall scarcely be any better off as evolving entities. The greatest necessity we have as souls is some kind of spiritual nucleus or power-point around which we can arrange a cosmic circle of consciousness by which everything we are able to experience at any angle or level of existence is relatable and workable. Given that vital factor, the rest lies in our hands, but without it we have little hope of spiritual success in any particular direction.

This is the nuclear age in more senses than one, and nuclear energy is of infinitely greater importance to us in spiritual dimensions than physical ones. We have to relearn how to harmonize ourselves around divine nil-nuclei, like a system around a sun, or perhaps like a cyclotron, so that we may derive the essential energy by which we live and exist directly from this source. Once it is firmly and definitely realized that such a spiritual power-point not only exists but IS existence emanating ITSELF of NIL, we have only to learn practical ways of relating with IT in order to put at least some fraction of such incredible power to good purpose through ourselves. The Quarterly Rites, by establishing links with this power-pattern, provide us with means of making this come true.

As in the case of all rites, these Quarterlies have an inner and an outer presentation which should be reflections of each other in their own spheres of influence. We might very well think of a properly conducted ritual as being like a portal or some means of access and communication between two states of being. To work correctly, a door has to be made so as to allow the passage of people in both directions. In the case of ritual, such a door has to operate for the mutual convenience of intelligent entities using very different types of consciousness and existing in extremely contrasting conditions of being. 'We', as humans, have the problem of constructing this door out of materials and means available to us which seem likely to lead *out* of our state *into* 'otherlife', and 'They' (whoever they are) have the same problem in theirs with regard to us. It is like an *Alice in Wonderland* mirror, with occupants of both rooms trying to reverse into each other's presence.

All we can do on our side of the 'veil' is to combine the various components of ritual procedure into patterns we believe ought to form a sort of key-structure which will penetrate not only the state of existence immediately behind our own but specific levels of inner life, and even reach specific intelligences. It is this element of selective choice as to the spiritual contact sought which makes magical rites what they are – operations of categorically directed inner will. Hence the necessity for designing them from constituent parts which have the property of leading our consciousness (and the energies with which they are linked) in whatever way is willed. With the Quarterlies, we are concerned with attuning ourselves to the Universal Spirit of creation from four particular points of the cosmic compass, and so all the physical accessories and effects are calculated to establish those precise relationships between the souls who seek and the Spirit which is sought.

The fair question is often asked, 'If constructive imaginative consciousness is of such importance, why can't we just imagine everything, and not bother with physical impedimenta like robes, incense, symbols, and the like?' The fair answer to this is, 'By all means, if the whole operation is meant for confinement to imaginative inner levels alone, and no effects are intended to manifest themselves in any way in this world.' This, of course, presents an obvious difficulty. Even if our intentions are of the very noblest, in terms of becoming better and more advanced souls, they are bound to have some sort of manifestation we could recognize here on earth, supposing any marked change of character took place. The physical links 'bringing through' such a phenomenon would be our own bodies, in which we live and present ourselves to each other. Since there have to be material linkages or 'mediums' in some form or another for any kind of inner energy to affect us on earth, the validity and practical usage of ritual symbolic patterns in shaping consciousness should be obvious. If we learn to perform rituals, for any purpose whatever, with effects that we ourselves can appreciate as earthly individuals, then we must take the trouble to provide paths for the energies to manifest.

There is no need to be over-elaborate in the provision of these physical path-symbols. Nothing whatever ought to be introduced into the workings of any rite without an entirely practical purpose, fully understood or intended by the operators. For example, any symbol of a decorative nature is only practical in so far as it assists consciousness to process itself for some particular purpose of will. If this is in keeping with, and essential to, the nature of the rite being worked, well and good. Otherwise it should not be present.

This is a very valuable rule indeed, and should always be observed, which is one reason why outdoor rites are so effective, climate permitting. Amid natural surroundings, which are symbols in themselves of the purest kind, only the absolutely necessary artifacts are normally set up. If a whole caravanserai of super-de-luxe modern camping equipment is included, the party might as well have hired a hotel convention room. Those unable to undertake rites without a conglomeration of personally-demanded extras should confine their activities entirely to circles of their own kind. A ritual is a very precise and properly-ordered construction indeed, and unless it is worked in the correct spirit, it will amount to no more than amateur theatricals. Even in that case it may still have value for all, providing their intentions are rightly directed.

These Quarterly Rites are therefore workable under almost any reasonable conditions, providing sincere efforts are made to cover the principal points, with appropriate symbology connecting inner and outer essentials. For instance, while it may not always be possible for the ritualists to be properly robed, they might at least make an attempt to wear something in keeping with the occasion, even if coloured cords, sashes or ribbons are all they can manage. It is the pattern and purpose of the rites which matter above all else, and the details of how to arrange the physically symbolic representations rest entirely with those who work them. Expensive equipment is no guarantee of a successful rite at all, but only of more fun facilities for those able to enjoy them. Ritualism is one human activity in which poor people very often have advantages over the rich, since they are frequently closer to the natural spirit in and with which rituals should be worked to achieve aims of inner importance.

If possible, some kind of ceremonial clothing ought to be worn by the Officers. The main consideration is colour, and the secondary one is style. Rules of plain good taste should decide this issue: and exotic or fantastic creations reminiscent of fancy dress balls are only likely to invite laughs at the expense of the wearer from human and other beholders. Failing any special design to requirements, the conventional habit or gown makes a reliable basic robe, and girdles with other additions may be suitably coloured. Mantles or flowing draperies are not recommended for practical reasons. Nothing, in fact, that is likely to catch on anything or trail around is advisable in rites of this nature. Care should especially be taken to wear nothing whatever of an inflammable kind.

With this type of rite, it is good standard practice to write out a list of every possible item which will be needed in physical form, and make it the responsibility of one official, usually the Cord, to be sure everything on the list is present and properly placed before the rite begins. This still does not absolve individual officers from checking their own necessities. Even in the event of any item being forgotten or failing in function, once the rite has started it must continue till the end without the circle being broken, and the deficiency should be got round in the most practical way, as part of the rite itself. This is a universal rule. Suppose, for instance, the fire is put out by a sudden downpour of rain. If it is possible to restart with available materials, this may be done while a song is sung, but otherwise the fire must be rebuilt in imagination only. Incidentally, should such an incident occur, the circle must still remain unbroken, and the companions would simply have to get wet through, unless provided with waterproof capes. Outdoor rites are subject to many hazards calling for all sorts of countermeasures and so, before being decided on, they should be very carefully catered for and considered. In the unlucky event of a rite being unavoidably broken off in mid-course by, for example, straying cows, or some insurmountable accident, it must be postponed for not less than a day, nor more than a month, and without fail worked through completely and correctly, even if this has to be done by a single companion of that circle on his own. Somehow or other the rite must be carried out once it has commenced its emergence into earthly expression.

The circle-dance is always a rather fascinating part of a ceremony, with a very ancient lineage of its own. It is far from being merely a childish game, but consists of a very exact piece of psychological and psychical procedure. Essentially, it is the action of 'dancing down' the unseen presence of the Inner One acting as a power-point for inner energies to be distributed through and around the circle. That is how the maypole dance was supposed to work in the days when people knew what they were doing with the symbol. The upright pole or staff represented the Divine One being invoked among the dancers. Each ribbon or cord stood for the contact between the individual dancers and the Deity. Their patterned processional dancing indicated that their relationships with each other through a commonly accepted circle of will formed the figure of the God (or telesmic image) around the staff at the centre. At the start they were relatively remote from each other, but as the action went on, they came closer and closer together until they were all in contact as one mass at the bottom of the staff, and the Divine One stood formed by their efforts in the midst of them. A truly wonderful and significant symbolic activity, the principles of which should be included in all seasonal ritual working.

Although these seasonal rites do not use a physical staff with ribbons, there is a physical central light or fire around which the dance is performed. The idea should be for each dancer to project his own idea of divinity in appropriate seasonal form like a light-line into the centre of the circle, and by cyclic combination with the others a telesmic image is constructed out of consciousness, which acts as a vehicle for the inner intelligence to work through. Just as a television picture is built up from many minute rods of light illuminating a screen with varying degrees of intensity, so a ritual telesmic image should be made from all the varying lines of Inner Light projected from the participants towards their common nuclear centre. While it is doubtful if this will materialize enough to be perceptible by physical eyes, an inner presence can very definitely be sensed by even average people, if a sufficiently sincere effort at invocation is made.

The general procedure of circle dancing is that the participants will first and foremost agree upon the sort of image or aspect to be invoked. In Spring, for instance, the figure might be that of a lovely young female, full of gaiety and life, with all the spiritual qualifications to be expected of a Vernal Divinity. Everyone will have his own ways of considering this concept, but as he goes round and round, he should try to create his idea in actuality as if he were walking or dancing around a real person and thinking about that person from every angle. This may even be done by imagining the sort of being under invocation as appearing in the middle of the circle and facing the direction of the Season. As the dancers travel around this creation, therefore, they will naturally view it and think about it from every degree of the compass, back, front and sides. By the time the dancing and chanting is finished, they ought to have at least a fair concept of what they were invoking, and more importantly, their invitation may be responded to, and a being may be with them in actuality as a focal point of inner intelligence. In ancient times, it was hoped that such an image would literally appear like a picture projected in the smoke which arose from the burning fire in the midst of the dancers. Who knows what they saw, or what indeed there is yet to see?

To facilitate this process, as the dance progressed, the dance leader called out or chanted some brief phrase or idea about the intelligence being invoked, and everyone else chanted back either the name of such a being, or some sonic evocation of it, usually a combination of vowel sounds, or sonorous and resonant noises which could be given any meaning at will. All this combined effort of consciousness in action around a single central idea does bring it positively into being among the invocants if they have genuine intentions in this direction and at least a reasonable notion of what they are doing. Circle chants should not be very difficult to arrange once the principles are understood. Here is a practical example of one intended to invoke divinity among dancers as a concept in its own right. The response-chant is simply a combination of the vowels arranged in the order of the Quarters and the I.O. call. The rhythm is lively and comparatively fast, so it makes a rather useful Spring circle-chant. It goes:

I am a void and the need of fulfilling,
EE I O AH-HU, EE I OH HO.
I am a thought and an effort of willing, etc.
I am a being and will to begin it, etc.
I am a mind and the thinking within it, etc.
I am an idea and its utmost abstraction, etc.
I am a self for its own satisfaction, etc.
I am a force and its centralization, etc.
I am a form and its manifestation, etc.
I am a light and its ray of reflection, etc.
I am a way and its path of direction, etc.
I am a word and the sound of it spoken, etc.
I am a sign and the truth of its token, etc.
I am a voice and the message it utters, etc.
I am a breath and the secret it mutters, etc.
I am an act and its primal causation, etc.
I am a rule and its best regulation, etc.
I am a belief and its basic foundation, etc.
I am a hope and its realization, etc.
I am an aim and its hidden intention, etc.
I am a notion and all its invention, etc.
I am a soul and the depth of its feeling, etc.
I am a hurt and the hope of its healing, etc.

I am a deed and the daring that did it, etc.
I am a fault and the mercy that hid it, etc.
I am a right and a reason for living, etc.
I am a wrong and the grace of forgiving, etc.
I am a smile and expression of gladness, etc.
I am a sigh and sensation of sadness, etc.
I am a dream and the solace of sleeping, etc.
I am a fear and the sorrow of weeping, etc.
I am a prayer and its silent petition, etc.
I am a remorse and the deepest contrition, etc.
I am a faith and its constant revision, etc.
I am a choice and a final decision, etc.
I am a life and the will of survival, etc.
I am a death and a sense of revival, etc.
I am a part of an ultimate union, etc.
I am the whole of an inner communion, etc.

(Gong or signal. All stop suddenly.)

WHOEVER YOU ARE, AND HOWEVER YOU TRY,
BE STILL AND CONSIDER, THE ONE THAT AM I.

Here the dancers look in centrally, and inwardly build up their figure among them as powerfully as they can.

Those are the principles behind the practice of circle-dancing. Naturally the actual rhythms and steps of a dance will vary according to season or purpose. In Springtime a light skipping movement, in Summer a firm, tapping tread, in Autumn a hearty jog, and in Winter a slow and steady measure. Ideally, the dancers ought to face centrally and dance sideways with hands held. Instead of this, they might remain in their positions of the circle and simply dance towards and back from the central point. There are many ways of arranging circle-dancing to suit requirements, and scripts are not difficult to write once the central idea emerges as it should. Practice in circle-dancing is essential for good working, and such practice must certainly be undertaken quite apart from any rite. It is unreasonable and unrealistic to expect good ritual workings without adequate rehearsal and trial.

This is especially so in the case of seasonal rites, where the participants might only meet on those few particular occasions.

Unless at least the Officers are prepared to meet more frequently than that and organize themselves and their rite into a fair condition of Cosmos, there is not much point in commencing what there is obviously no real will to continue properly. There are few fiascos more stupid than a lot of people not knowing what they are supposed to do and losing interest in the proceedings as these become more muddled. This is bound to happen unless the rules of the rites are carefully observed. None should be admitted to the rites except those trained to work them, or their equivalents, and they must be responsible individuals who may be relied on to the full within the realms of human capability. Anyone taking the attitude, 'oh, yes, of course I'll be there', with a mental reservation of 'unless something more interesting turns up, or I feel like doing something different' should be firmly excluded from any circle intending to do really solid work among its members.

The sole secret of building up any useful sort of circle is to get the central nucleus correctly related first, and the rest will steadily cosmate around it. A badly balanced or ineffective nucleus inevitably leads to disaster or plain failure. Unless the Officers and their central spiritual contact are properly balanced with each other and fulfilling all their functions, no circle is true nor will it ever be worth increasing. Granted it is an exceptionally difficult and discouraging project among 'occultly'-minded people to find and keep in operative contact a minimum of four individual souls capable of forming a correct cosmic relationship with each other and continuing in effective harmony. Just how difficult and discouraging, no one could possibly realize who has not attempted such a task. It is a salutary spiritual exercise of a unique kind. Nevertheless if it takes a whole lifetime, the effort should be maintained until some sort of success seems to be approaching – and it will only come after considerable expenditure of time and trouble.

Precisely why so many small 'occult' groups fail as they do with monotonous regularity is a multi-sided matter to be considered at much greater length than is possible here. The single factor emerges that those constituting such groups or circles are obviously not seeking genuine spiritual light with the same singleness of will they employ in their ordinary lives to obtain money or achieve other material objectives. No average human being with a living to earn or a career to consider can possibly be expected to keep his attention on high spiritual matters the whole of his time. What may fairly be demanded is that he will devote his wholehearted true will to the cosmic cause for convenient periods at definite intervals. It is regularity and depth of devotion which are of most importance. The Quarterly Rites make only four definite demands in an entire year. On each occasion, the ritualists are enjoined to lay aside material preoccupations and stand up in their own right as souls seeking their source and aligning themselves with the natural energies of their existence. They are invited, as it were, to take a brief holiday from the selves they show the world, and become acquainted with the true selves of their inner life.

Despite all this, it would be a great mistake to consider the Quarterly Rites as purely religious occasions, or even religious at all in the sense in which many people might interpret the word. They are essentially acts of relationship between human beings and whatever they believe to be the cosmic cause in which they hope to continue as souls. The number of different ways of establishing this relationship depends on the human abilities and the scope of the soul involved. It is the intention or will to experience such a relationship which makes it possible for us. We could actually do it in any way we liked, even with the most commonplace methods. We could strike a match, open a book – in fact do anything at all, and put whatever inner meaning or intention of will we chose into the act. That is ritual. The Quarterly Rites consist of much more than the words and activities we have been considering. They are occasions not only for souls to communicate with inner beings, but also with each other in the most direct way by personal contact. Those who are likely to practise rites such as these should have much to gain from each other's experience. In olden times, the great feasts, as they were called, were no hasty affairs, but gatherings lasting up to several days. A lot happened in that time, not a great deal of which would nowadays be classed as purely religious practice.

Of course in those far-off days people did not make any particular distinctions between 'religious' or 'non-religious' activities. They and their divinities were bound together into one life no matter what took place. They did not adopt any holy and pious attitudes to cover themselves with when approaching deities. They just were themselves and that was that. Whether they ate, drank, spoke, laughed, wept, raged, sorrowed, or behaved in any human way, their divinities shared all this with them as a natural part of life. When man started locking up his deities in secret temples and conveniently losing the keys, humanity as a whole lost what has not yet been replaced – innocence. It was a bad error when man became so aware of his own faults that he guiltily divided himself into two categories, offering the best side to the gods, and the worst to his fellow humans. Such was our 'Fall', or 'Knowledge of Good and Evil'. Only the 'Fruit of the Living Tree', or enough wisdom gained through innumerable human incarnations is likely to repair the damage and raise us to the spiritual status we ought otherwise to have achieved long since.

The Quarterly Rites should provide us with some opportunities for being ourselves with ourselves in the spirit of all selves as One. There ought to be enough time allowed for friendliness, conversation, enjoyment, and the general pleasure people of common circles of consciousness are able to offer to each other. This is just as much an integral part of the rites as the scripted words and procedures, and possibly even more important. The practice to avoid if possible is to turn the rites into hurried affairs crammed into a single meeting of an hour or so while people's minds are concerned with timetables or transport, or, worse still, try to sandwich the rite between two other engagements. Those unprepared to treat the rites as they deserve should never participate in them.

Essentially, the rites are friendly and intimate affairs between well-intentioned entities of human and other states of being. They should be celebrated as such and thoroughly enjoyed from all angles. Modern life being what it is, the style of the proceedings may be rather cramped, but the minimum of a weekend should be devoted to each Quarterly Rite. Those able to convene for the entire time ought to do so, and others must do the best they can with available means. People who cannot imagine what to do in each other's company for even a few hours are quite unsuited to the rites anyway. A really poor system of working the rites was used by one group whose members were expected to arrive with just sufficient time to robe up in solemn silence, go through a somewhat severe version of a rite with no music or joy whatever, and depart immediately afterwards with a minimum of contact between them. The idea was to 'eliminate fallible human elements and false appearances of personality', thus being able to concentrate alone on the 'high, pure and spiritual'. Presumably the survivors of such a system found some twisted sort of satisfaction in their gloomy gatherings, and if this was indeed their true will, why should they be denied their rights? Unto each his own.

There is so much to be had out of the rites if they are done even moderately well, that those who practise them regularly would rather forego almost anything else. Apart from the human company and pleasure of friendly companionship, there is an extraordinary sense of personal inner satisfaction which has to be experienced in order to be understood. It is very difficult to describe accurately, being far deeper and truer than mere self-importance, since it is rather more of an inner knowledge and conviction beyond doubt of the real value and use of each single soul-self, for what it *is*, in its relationship to the infinite entity. By means of the rites we learn to KNOW OURSELVES, as the Ancient Mysteries enjoined all true initiates. We come to feel part of Cosmos itself, and valuable parts too! Such knowledge is priceless.

All normal aspiring souls want to feel themselves not only as individual entities, but as essential and necessary integers of some larger combinations of consciousness. This has a naturally expansive effect on their own being, adding considerably to their personal status as people. The average human being is usually content to feel himself centred firstly in himself, then his family and friends, and after those circles, in consecutively wider ones such as business concerns, social groupings, political and religious associations, then perhaps national, ethnical, or even world-wide networks. The wider the circle, the more remote does it feel to the little human soul in the middle. Few really believe they can personally influence the destiny of a nation, or alter religious outlooks as a whole. Yet these do change, and some kind of consciousness is obviously responsible. When it comes to the natural forces and phenomena around us, such as the solar system, the seasons, time, space, and the events we experience by just living amongst all this existence, how many of us truly feel and know ourselves to be not only shareholders in this incredible company of consciousness, but also eligible for a directorship as well? How often do we feel that the mysterious happenings behind our beings are not merely inexorable energies pushing us around regardless of our inclinations, but are also things we can do ourselves in our own way, affairs we are closely concerned with, and issues at stake in which we have even a considerable say, once we learn the language? To achieve at least some measure of this natural majesty is the major motive of the seasonal and other rites.

Our ancestors knew how to feel one with nature herself. If wind blew, they blew with it. Should fire warm, so did they. In the sea they became as water, on earth solid and fertile. They accepted the elements of existence and *lived* them. How far do we live real lives today in our factories, offices, shops, and other artificial environments? Are the circles of commercial, political, social and other systems adequate substitutes for the Cosmic circles to which our beings are basically bound? Surely our greatest need as souls is to outgrow all artificial limits save those we impose upon ourselves for the sake of encouraging this very growth? Mankind may plunge into sheer materialism as deeply as he likes, or hide his finer instincts behind a disguise of 'humanitarianism' as much as he pleases, but fundamentally the animating principle of humanity is spiritual in nature. Unless this principle achieves some kind of working relationship with its own equivalents in the rest of creation, man cannot become a fully functioning creature of consciousness. A number of human beings attempt and even achieve some measure of this vital relationship by means of the different religious systems, but it seems only too obvious that a very large proportion of the human race are rightly or wrongly unwilling to try this, and a small but very important minority of advancing individuals are seeking rather different lines of approach to the problem from those that any of the established faiths have to offer. The Christian Church in particular appears very conscious of this deficiency, but in attempting to alter itself so as to meet modern requirements, it is only damaging its structure in spiritual dimensions to quite a serious degree.

At this period of human evolution on this planet, man is undergoing a transition from one level of living to another in more than material ways, and everything is in a fairly rapid state of alteration – whether for better or worse, only our future will prove. Our spiritual standards and concepts especially are shaken to a state of considerable uncertainty. Yet unless we manage to find firm and definite fulcra for our spiritual faith, we shall find nothing that makes even the most affluent human life really worth living. We cannot begin to construct our circles of inner consciousness without the prerequisite fixed central point which determines the circumference. However we term it, and despite our refusals to recognize its nature, this fixed point is the principle of divinity inherent in all manifestation. If we work from that, we shall make sense for and to ourselves in any direction we please. Otherwise we simply wander around pointlessly.

The Quarterly Rites outlined are only modern adaptions of mankind's oldest and deepest faith – in himself and divinity related by a common spirit and capable of united expression of entity via mutual fields of energy. Put into crude terms, man says in his heart, 'Whoever you are, there's thee and me, and we had best do something about it.' All faiths are extensions, elaborations and decorations of this fundamental fulcrum. The Christian Church uses it as the Trinity of Father, Son and Holy Ghost, or God, Man and Spirit, adding itself as the fourth issue. Other faiths arrange it differently, and the Quarterly Rites afford opportunities for participants to arrange it for themselves, which, in the end, is exactly what all of us are expected to do. We are slowly turning in our great circle. Originally, mankind had to discover divinity for himself as best he might, then for a long time he followed made-up systems and remained satisfied with them, now we are getting back to the stage when we have to find our own faiths again on new inner levels. Back to square one on a different layout of life, in fact. We may as well adopt equivalent methods to those which served us well enough in time gone by, and Quarterly Rites are truly time-tested affairs.

There is no authoritative ruling that the rites must infallibly be worked exactly in the forms specified in the previous section of this book. They are intended for use by all who find them practical and beneficial and have no particular means or reason for making up their own. They have already served with good effect in the past, and are perfectly capable of offering even better service in the future. So far as is humanly possible, they have built-in safeguards against evil or improper influences. All the best ritual elements have been incorporated somewhere in their structure, and they are both simple and beautiful to work, allowing a very fair proportion of do-it-yourself ritualism within their framework. To a certain extent, this is a rather welcome innovation, and one likely to gain ground in future practice. In principle, the fixed parts of the rites provide the leads and opportunities for the operators to introduce their own personal and individual wills in a variety of ways. Thus the rituals are as much or as little as anyone intends them to be, which is a great advantage to most workers.

It will be noted that each rite, quite apart from its invocations, formulae, etc., contains some particular dramatic activity for the externalization of energy, and a special typified meditation for internalizing consciousness in order to make contact with inner intelligence. The activities are planting for Spring, washing and anointing for Summer, reaping for Autumn, and reflecting for Winter. The meditations are associated with symbols representing the state of nature at that period, with which some kind of personal affinity is sought. They are to indicate that we should look into ourselves in that particular light, and discover what is revealed to us in that way. A great deal may be accomplished by this procedure if sufficient trouble is taken with the symbolic arrangements and the meditational work done by their means.

The general procedure with this type of internalizing intelligence is to take the externality of the symbol as it stands, form a concept around it, then push this inside oneself to a point where it disappears into nil. If contact can still be held with that point successfully, a responding symbol should emerge into the field of awareness for consideration by the enquiring consciousness. Whatever this symbol may be, it ought to be noted down without fail as soon as possible, so that it may be recalled and examined subsequently at leisure. No attempt should be made to interpret it as it 'comes through', because this would interrupt and most likely prevent its arrival into awareness. Whatever is 'received' during a quarterly ritual meditation will in all probability have some overall meaning for the period ahead, and may very well be a valuable guide or source of inspiration. It is not usually wise for the recipient of such impressions to tell anyone else what these were. Both the petitions and any 'messages' received during the meditations are entirely personal between the human and the Other end of Awareness exchanging these confidences.

The so-called 'passwords' are meditational key-phrases which are supposed to grow up with the year, out of each other, as if they were living things in their own right. An initial idea is 'planted' in the Spring like a seed, improved in Summertime like a flower, gathered in Autumn as harvest, and cleared into another condition during the Winter. Ideas will do in their dimensions just what materials will do in a physical state. Suppose we divide any natural process into four, such as: acorn—oak tree—timber—furniture. We might take any acorn and see the most wonderful furniture in it, given the factors of time and events. In the same way, an initial idea may grow into very practical results by natural development through normal cosmic stages. All we have to do is to think 'If this idea is a seed, how would it look as a flower, then as a fruit, and finally as a finished end-product?' In the case of our rites, we are allowing sufficient time and events for each stage to evolve from the last. Thus it is important not to choose the passwords greatly in advance of the rite itself. They should most definitely come of their own accord at the right time as a result of nearly three months' growth in the fertile soil of the subconscious mind.

This process is bound to take place in the awareness of everyone within the circle of the rites, but obviously there has to be a one-for-all key-phrase. Finding this to mutual satisfaction may not be an easy matter. Perhaps the plan might be followed of writing a number of suitable phrases on slips and choosing one by lot in the Spring. Everyone could submit his own in that way, and whether or not his was the chosen phrase, he should follow it in private appropriately to each season in turn. In the Summer, the same procedure would be used to select a slip with the idea developed by everyone to a 'flower stage', and so with the other two seasons. Such a means of selection certainly makes for shared consciousness among the group, and also introduces the element of the unexpected, often in quite interesting and pleasing ways.

It should scarcely be necessary to say that some kind of a record ought to be made in order to estimate progress, or discover ideas for future improvements. Long or wordily written reports are both uncalled for and unwanted. The briefest outline of salient points, such as attendance list, general conditions, incidental occurrences, the password chosen, a copy of any address made, plus whatever particular remarks seem called for, is quite sufficient. It is a help if everyone will take the trouble to write his personal impressions of the rite, so that these may be evaluated by the member of the group best qualified for such a task. What is really needed are accurate accounts of how the rites affect individuals from within, and how their lives may be altered in any way because of participation in the ritual workings. In other words, the reactive results in terms of personal experience. By summing up and extracting the essence of such vital information, the rites may really be appreciated for what they are and what they actually mean to those working them. This, after all, is surely what truly matters most of all.

Once these Quarterly Rites are set in operation properly, they will gather momentum almost of their own accord, and providing they are reasonably regulated by common sense, can only be beneficial to all concerned. The main thing is to make a start, and let the rest grow naturally from its origin. There is no reason why anyone should wait around hopefully for other suitable souls before commencing the rites. They can be worked quite practically by one person. We should bear in mind that the Cosmos we live in was commenced by and controlled with a single supreme Consciousness. If the Ultimate had waited for another like Itself before beginning to BE, we ourselves would certainly never have been. If we intend to imitate Its behaviour in our own small ways, then we shall have to follow the fourfold rule of magic – KNOW, WILL, ACT, and KEEP COUNSEL. Thus far has knowledge been given. Now who will act upon it so that counsel may indeed be kept among Companions of the Light? None are excluded from even the highest cosmic circles save those who will not seek admission, and there is only one way in. Each through his own gate. Who comes his way upon the course of cosmos?

✝

Opening and Closing a Rite

✝

Opening and Closing a Rite

*I*T was not originally intended to include in this work the ritual details which follow. They are not exactly secret, but belong to the private workings of one particular Circle which habitually uses the Four Seasonal Rites we have been dealing with. Nevertheless, after considerable thought it seemed reasonable to offer these procedures purely as examples to work from, when formulating rituals for individual and Group usage. Let it be entirely understood that the action and effort of making up Rites is in itself a Rite of the highest importance. Making up our own rituals is the very essence of Magic itself, providing these accord with good fundamental base-patterns. Still, when learning the art, it is undoubtedly valuable to have examples of other people's customs and practices. Therefore, it has been finally decided to put forward these very individualized little rituals with the sincere hope that they may help others arrange their own.

Since the Circle in question had some connections with both the Qabalistic and the Celtic Traditions, the Rites were given the overall title of: 'Opening and Closing in the Universal Degree'. This meant that they served as a general commencement and completion ceremony for whatever type of Rite right be worked in that circle. The custom was that the Principal Officer would intone the major portions, and the others respond, but there is no reason at all why the verbal sections should not be apportioned to whoever is best fitted for their recitation.

Briefly, the members of the Circle entered the Place of Working in their proper order so that they came to their appointed Stations in deosil fashion. The one 'free' member who moved around in accordance with needs was the 'Officer of the Cord'. This personage acted as Doorkeeper, Messenger, or Bearer of whatever might be called for in the course of a Rite. The Principal Officers of the Stations only left their positions for very specific reasons, unless the whole Circle had to circumambulate. When the Circle had settled into position, the Principal began:

Principal: Companions, we are come together with a will to work and worship in accordance with the Law by which we live in Light: O Perfect Love – DO WHAT *THOU* WILT.

ALL: O Perfect Love – DO WHAT *THOU* WILT.

Principal: Let us prove ourselves, then exclude whom or whatsoever is unfitted to remain within our Circle.

(Here everyone had to give their proper 'sign', usually a manual gesture to indicate their initiatory status or entitlement for inclusion in the Circle. Though normally a pure formality, it should never be omitted.)

Principal: Truly we are proved Companions. Let us now be purified from all that is unworthy in this place or in our persons. Our minds and souls must be most properly prepared if we hold hopes of gaining grace or goodness by our present thoughts and actions. May the Mercy of the All-Compassionate be moved among us.

Officer of West: O Spirit of Eternal Verity, in Whom all hearts are open, minds are known, and souls discerned, put us we pray, at Peace in Thee with one another. Expel from us our evils, and forgive our faults as we now exorcise ourselves and purify this dedicated place. In the Name of the Wisdom, the Love, the Justice, and the Infinite Mercy of the One Eternal Spirit. AMEN.

(Circle Cross Sign made, holy water sprinkled from WEST, gong sounded, and short silence observed.)

West *(cont.)*: Companions, we are purified. Now let us be protected both by Fire and Sword before the Outer Portals.

(Here the CORD places Emblems or actualities of a lighted lamp and sword by the left and right side of the Doorway respectively while directions are given by the Officers concerned.)

South: Be the Torch of Truth and Everlasting Light our sure deliverance from every Darkness and deception. In the Name, etc.

East: Be the Sword of spiritual strength and discipline our sure defence against all evils and antagonisms. In the Name, etc.

North: Companions, we are under the protection of Divine Omnipotence. Let us arrange ourselves according to our Pattern of Perfection, the Encircled Cross. Be its Points, Pivots, and Perimeter, proclaimed around the Power of its most Secret Spiritual Centre.

ALL: Above us – LIGHT.   Below us – LIFE.
Around us – LAW.   Within us – LOVE.
SO MOTE IT BE. AMEN.

Principal: Blessed be the Ancient Four of our Foundation and the Cosmic Cord of their connection. Let these relate themselves the Way of Light.

(Here the respective Officers take up their proper ceremonial Symbols in turn, and individually circumambulate the Circle slowly while bearing them. Sometimes members of the Circle touch each Symbol as it passes them by. When each Officer has completed the circuit, and placed their Symbol in whatever position it will occupy for the rest of the Rite, they proclaim its purpose accordingly:)

East: Sure and devoted is our Sword upheld in Air as truest token of our Faith.

South: Heaven and Earthward points our Rod before the Fire as truest token of our Hope.

West: Compassionate and cheerful is our Cup above the Water as truest token of our Love.

North: Secure and steadfast is our Shield upon the Earth as truest token of our Work.

Cord: Confident and certain is our Cord conjoining us as truest token of our Consciousness.

Principal: Blessed be the Symbols and the Signs whereby our minds and souls work willingly together in the Spirit of Eternal Understanding manifested through the Holy Mysteries.

THE CHARGES

(These may be all given by the PRINCIPAL – who may be any of the Four Officers, but customarily is the Officer of the South – or by the Officers of the Stations themselves.)

East: Let Sword be sharp and ever keen
To save us from all things unclean.
South: Let Rod be rulership of Right
To guide us in our Way of Light.
West: Let Cup be charged with competence
To fill us with benevolence.
North: Let Shield be adequate and sure
To keep us faithful and secure.
Cord: Let Cord be fixed or free at Will
To compass all we know with skill.
Principal: Sword SAVE. Rod RULE.
Cup CARE. Shield SUSTAIN.
Cord CONNECT.
So let us live in Light together in this Circle of the Cosmic Cross.

(Gong. Silence.)

Cord: Let us be provided with a worthy purpose for our present practice.
Principal: Be it proclaimed by us all concerned both Inwardly and Outwardly that our Intention is ...

(Here the Intention of the Rite is stated in brief conclusive terms.)

ALL: SO MOTE IT BE. AMEN.
Principal: May the Blessing of the Mighty Ones be truly with us now and evermore in all that we accomplish or attempt. In the Name, etc.

PASSING THE PILLARS

(Here a visualization is made of the Gateway to the Inner Kingdom opening and everyone finding their own Way Within.)

Cord: Be the Inner Portals opened, that we may proceed with Power upon our Path between its Pillars.

East: Blessed be the Left Hand Pillar that defines our limits on the Way of Light.

South: Blessed be the Right Hand Pillar that prevents our passage to the Way of Darkness.

West: Blessed be the Middle Way that leads us into true Illumination.

North: In Faith we seek. In Hope we knock *(knocks signal on floor)*. In loving confidence we ask the Supreme Spirit of our Guidance:

From the unreal – lead us to the REAL.

From the false – lead us to the TRUTH.

From the darkness – lead us into LIGHT.

PROCESSION

(Here all circumambulate around the Circle reciting or chanting:)

ALL: Through the East South West and North,
We seek the Way of Light set forth.
Dawn, Noon, Dusk, and Midnight hour
We spiral round our Point of Power.
Fire and Water, Earth and Air
Show the Elements we bear.
Sword and Rod. Cord. Cup and Shield
Are the Symbols that we wield.
God Above and Man below,
Around our Cosmic Cross we go.
EE AI OH AH HU-OO.

(This vowel chant is kept up for several circlings, getting softer each time until the PRINCIPAL stops the action at a point where the Officers are at Stations, and says:)

Principal: Companions, we are duly proven, purified, protected and empowered to put our present purpose into practice. With Divine permission let us now proceed. In the Name, etc.

At this point the main Rite itself commences. This might mean an entire rearrangement of the Circle into another formation, and everyone must know in advance what he or she is supposed to do. All changes should be made with a minimum of movement and disturbance. Adequate rehearsal and practice is essential to obtain this proficiency in neat and effective action. The Rite of Commencement ought to have provided 'lift' for the participants to arrive at the necessary Inner condition of readiness to engage in the major working. In a way, the principle of this is very similar to the initial thrust behind a rocket ship which puts it into orbit. Providing the first stage falls off properly and allows the remainder to take up its orbit in a correct fashion, all is well. Analogically in our Ritual working, we have to disengage from the impetus of the Commencement section, and settle into the main Ritual orbit with a maximum of ease and efficiency. This is only possible if everything has been planned and arranged in advance right down to small details. Good Ritualists should always aim for what amounts to professional skill in their art.

When the main Rite is done, a sort of 'descent programme' is needed to bring the ritualists back to ordinary Earth levels of life with a series of broad 're-entry' circles that culminate in what we might describe as a perfect landing. Thus, the psyche is gently and naturally brought back into alignment with the everyday personality without shock or sense of estrangement with its customary environments. It is most important that ritualists should not leave their place of working in a highly 'charged' or 'exalted' state of soul. This is asking for trouble. All should leave their working area or Circle in the same 'normal' condition with which they should have entered it. Hence the necessity for a graduated 'letdown' after any form of major rite. Really expert ritualists can accomplish this for themselves with a few rapid Inner adjustments, but it is always wise to have a standard procedure for general use by any operative Circle. Thus all members are likely to develop the good habit of proper closure when they work Rites by themselves, and are certain to observe it in company with others.

The Closure Ceremony we shall follow here is entitled:

CLOSING IN THE UNIVERSAL DEGREE

Principal: In the Name, etc.

Companions, let us change our course of consciousness from these activities of Inner Life to our mundane affairs among mankind on ordinary living levels. Be it borne in mind each state of being reflects the other through our attitudes and actions in them. May we be worthy mediators of the Holy Spirit which conjoins all Life as One within its Sacred Cosmic Circle.

As above – so below.

As within – so without.

As in Heaven – so on Earth.

As with God – so with Man.

Forever and forevermore. Amen.

ALL: SO MOTE IT BE. AMEN.

Principal *(cont.)*: Let us proclaim Peace with Power between ourselves and all the Angles of Existence. Be there Peace between us and the Highest.

ALL: SO MOTE IT BE. AMEN.

Cord: Be there Peace between us and the Lowest.

ALL: SO MOTE IT BE. AMEN.

East: Be there Peace between us and the East.

ALL: SO MOTE IT BE. AMEN.

South: Be there Peace between us and the South.

ALL: SO MOTE IT BE. AMEN.

West: Be there Peace between us and the West.

ALL: SO MOTE IT BE. AMEN.

North: Be there Peace between us and the North.

ALL: SO MOTE IT BE. AMEN.

Principal: Be there Peace among us in our Hearts.

ALL: SO MOTE IT BE. AMEN.

(During this, those concerned may make appropriate Signs to the Quarters named.)

West: Let us commend to the Divine Compassion those in sickness or affliction whom we are unable to assist by mortal means.

(A short silence for prayer or meditation.)

West *(cont.):* O Thou ever-loving One of Might and Mercy, be unto these souls, and all who suffer, their Divine deliverance from present perils. May they truly be made whole, and kept within the Circle of Thy care for every creature.

ALL: SO MOTE IT BE. AMEN.

North: Be the Blessed Dead remembered, who are bound with us by links of love through Everlasting life.

(Short silence.)

May these, and all true souls, find Peace and their complete fulfilment in the Light Divine Forevermore.

ALL: SO MOTE IT BE. AMEN.

East: Let us link ourselves with other souls in this, and every world, who stand within our Circle of Companionship because of faith and friendship in our common Cosmic cause.

(Short silence.)

May true fraternity and fellowship increase among, and bring together, all believers in the Holy Mysteries of Earth and Heaven.

ALL: SO MOTE IT BE. AMEN.

Principal: Our work is done. Our Will made one.

Let us set right our Signs of Light.

(Here the Symbols are restored to their original places, being circumambulated by each Officer before final placement.)

North: Blessed be the steady Shield.

That keeps us firm in every field.

East: Blessed be the faithful Sword

That guards us with due watch and ward.

South: Blessed be the righteous Rod

That guides us truly unto God.

West: Blessed be the loving Cup

That lifts our souls and spirits up.

Cord: Blessed be the constant Cord

That binds us into one accord.

(Chant)

ALL: So Mote it be indeed.

Our Cosmic Cross proclaimed.

All that our spirits need
Within its Pattern framed.
Let us live as it shows
With conduct that is right.
While Wisdom in us grows
Toward the One True Light.
AMEN.

East: In Peace we came together, and in peace did we remain of one mind, in one place, at one time. Peacefully now let us part from one another that our ways may meet in peace again. Be a blessing bidden on our going forth.

South: Thanks be to the Eternal One and our appointed guardians for what has passed in peace among us in this Sacred Circle. May the benefits therefrom come not to us alone, but unto all Mankind besides. In the Name, etc. *(Short silence.)*

West: Each to their proper place in Peace proceed, and as our present Circle ceases its formation, may the Forces focused here flow freely forth and find fulfilment through the will within the Word.

I. A. O. AMEN. *(Gong stroke.)*

(This phrase is chanted resonantly, and echoed by all, while turning on their places rightwardly for a full pivoted circle.)

North: Let us be at silent ease together. We may not at the shrine remain while work awaits us in the Outer World to be accomplished by the Holy Will within us. Therefore close all Inner Portals carefully with due acknowledgment toward their faithful Guardians.

(Here everyone makes closing gestures upon themselves and returns Inner thanks as they see fit.)

Principal: Unfasten now the Outer Gateway leading to our mortal mundane lives.

(The securing Symbols are removed from the Door, and it is unlocked or set open.)

Principal *(cont.):* Blessed are the eyes that are enlightened.
   Blessed are the ears that hear the Truth.
   Blessed are the lips of guarded speech.
   Blessed is the heart that holds Compassion.
   Blessed are the hands of kindly friendship.
   Blessed are the feet that walk with Wisdom.
   Now in Perfect Love: BE AS THOU WILT.
   In the Name, etc.

After this, everyone files quietly out of the place and disrobes in another room or some distance from the working area. It is not, as a rule, a good idea to start chattering away like mad until after at least any regalia, marks of office, or other insignia on the persons of the participants have been put away properly. Then, too, after each Rite, someone must be responsible for clearing things up, restoring the place to a normal condition, and generally putting all to rights. This should be done with a minimum of fuss or confusion. When this essential work is finished, everyone can let their hair down and enjoy each other's company in an ordinary manner.

It is good practice to confine the 'Inner affairs and confidences' of any Circle strictly within the Circle itself while it is formally and ceremonially operative. Thus, matters dealt with or discussed among members while the Circle is ritually in action should never be brought up or referred to outside those conditions. If it should be really necessary to tackle some particular point concerning the affairs of the Circle, then a proper quorum of accredited members must be duly formed between them with a rapid formula such as:

'In the Name, etc. We constitute this Circle of Companionship among us for the special purpose of ... *(whatever it may be).* SO MOTE IT BE. AMEN.'

The important point arising here, is that nothing whatever must be dealt with by that Circle *except* the single matter it was constituted to deal with. Everything must be kept to that one point. This effectively concentrates energy into a force-focus which can be directed toward the issue in question. Should other new affairs come to light during that particular Circle-session, as they probably will, these are best left for the attention of a fresh Circle-constitution altogether. At the end of each such Circle-session a rapid dissolution formula can be used, such as:

'In the Name, etc. We close this Circle of Companionship among us on Earth, that it may continue unto its conclusion in the Higher Consciousness of Heaven. SO MOTE IT BE. AMEN.'

Ritual formulations of some kind ought always to be made when activities concerned with Circle-affairs are undertaken. This applies whether the Circle consists of one single soul, or any greater number of living entities.

Although it is really best for everyone to construct or use his or her own formulae for blessings and consecrations, some examples may not come entirely amiss for those in search of ideas. We will take four typical specimens employed for consecrating the Elements. First the Air.

AIR △

'In the Beginning, did the Holy Spirit issue from the Void and breathe a vital, living soul into Mankind. May we also breathe forth Words which act throughout our Inner atmosphere, and bring to life our latent spiritual qualities.

We call upon Thee, O thou source of Inspiration filling us with faith that we shall find our final and Immortal freedom in the Spheres of Spirit. Speak unto our souls that we may hold the echoes of thy harmony. Enter into this, thine ambient Element that it may bear for us thy vibrant voice ... *(here suitable gestures or actions are made)* ... Manifest thy meaning for us, that the winds of Truth will wake us with thy messages, and may the Angels of the Air become apparent to our eyes of Inner vision.

Be thou consecrated, faithful creature of the Air, through the Power, and in the service of, the One Eternal Life whose single breaths we surely are. AMEN.'

FIRE △

'Let there be LIGHT no Darkness may extinguish. Burn evermore, thou Fire of Love that ripens every spiritual Seed.

107

In the separation of thine essence from thy substance lies the Work of Wisdom. Thou art strongest of the strong, overcoming subtlety and interpenetrating all solidity. In thine adaption is the Arcane art, and secret of the Sacred Science.

We call upon Thee, O Father of All, radiant with thine illuminating rays. O unseen Parent of the Sun, pour forth thy life-giving power and energize thy Divine Spark. Enter into this flame and let it be agitated by the breath of the Most Holy Spirit ... *(here flame is lit or gestures made)* ... Manifest thy power and open for us the Hidden Temple which is concealed within this flame. May we become regenerated by thy Light, and the breadth, height, fullness and Crown of Solar Radiance appear, so that God Within shines forth.

Be thou consecrated, faithful creature of the Fire, through the Power, and in the service of, that Supreme LIGHT Whose single sparks we surely are. AMEN.'

WATER ▽

'Let there be a firmament in the midst of the waters so that Sea and Sky may separate into themselves. That which is above is like to that which is below for the appearance of a single wonder. The Sun is its Father, the Moon its Mother, and the Wind has carried it into conception. It ascends from Earth to Heaven, and descends to Earth again when it is due.

We call upon thee, O thou Mighty Mother of Whose womb comes everlasting Life. Maiden of the Mysteries art thou, and nurse of all that lives by means of Nature. Enter into this, thine Element of Water, moving it for us by thy Compassion ... *(here water is salted or just blessed with a gesture)* ... Manifest for us thy potency and open unto us the hidden depths of Wisdom. May we savour whatsoever we experience therein with the appreciative salt of good sound sense, and let all tides, waves, and currents of the Cosmic Ocean bear our consciousness toward the anchorage of our eventual Attainment.

Be thou consecrated, faithful creature of the Water, through the power, and in the service of, that Universal Sea of Spirit Whose particular and scattered drops we surely are. AMEN.'

EARTH ▽

'Of slime and clay did the Creative Spirit form the flesh and bones of Man, our bodies being of rich red Earth and particles of dust. May we manifest through matter with true Wills that we shall ultimately rise to be the rightful rulers and administrators of this Outer Kingdom we experience in ordinary living.

We call upon thee by thine olden and beloved Name, O Mother Earth. Thine is our field of present life, and by thine aid do we remain the human beings we are. Enter into this, thine Element of Earth, and stabilize us with thy firm solidity ... *(here the Earth is signed, or gestures made)* ... Manifest for us the meaning of those special secrets we must learn in order to observe thy laws, and find our purpose on this planet. May we truly grow from being Children of Creation into loyal and faithful subjects of the Supreme Living Spirit.

Be thou consecrated, faithful creature of the Earth, through the Power, and in the service of, that solitary Self-Existing One, Whose single atoms we most surely are. AMEN.

BLESSING THE BREAD OR SOLID EUCHARISTIC SYMBOL

'Blessed be unto Divinity and all of us, our body of belief we share together which unites us unto one another for the sake of loving kindness.

May this special Sign with which we seek to feed our faith, sustain our souls to an immortal Life in Spirit. In the Name,' etc.

BLESSING THE WINE, OR LIQUID EUCHARISTIC SYMBOL

'Blessed be unto Divinity and all of us, that Cup of Consciousness wherein the essence of Eternal Entity, and our awareness of It, meet and mingle for the sake of Life in one another.

May this special Sign by which we hope to realize our true Identity, communicate to us the Holy Presence we now humbly seek within our secret hearts. In the Name,' etc.

Sometimes it is a good plan to have parts of the Rites in music or speech on tape so that these may be fitted in where necessary. Thus it is possible for those who cannot be present in person to participate in a Rite to some extent, or make their contribution to its intellectual content. Short recorded messages from other Circles give a wonderful sense of fellowship and linkage with those forming their own Groups along the same lines elsewhere. Also, some tape material is useful to have as a standby in case someone fails to attend a Circle, and an unexpected gap has to be filled at short notice from otherwise insufficient material. One might almost say that a sound tape-recorder is a most necessary item of equipment for any modern Circle. The background effects of a Circle-Dance, for instance, or even the Dance itself in full, goes very well on tape. In this way, people who may be unfamiliar or uncertain with the words and actions can simply concentrate on following the chant around and taking sense of it as this comes. Those who know the words may join in where they please, and everyone will feel free to interpret the circumambulations in their own fashion. The Zodiac Chant, given here as a specimen, is written for ordinary plain-chant rhythm, and is meant to be taken at a steady and regular rate. In slow time it is most suitable for the Winter Season, but of course could easily be used for other occasions.

THE ZODIAC CIRCLE-CHANT

1. ARIES ♈

'O Ram of Heaven, open thou our pilgrimage. Break down the barriers upon our Path, and lead us into active living; enter in the Sign of fiery Faith and sacrifice, so may our hearts be filled with courage that we may persist unflinchingly until our journey's ending.'

2. TAURUS ♉

'Thou Bull of Earth be strong and patient. May we learn of thee endurance in our working and our waiting; be thy horns to us an ancient sign of holy exaltation, and thy fertility a source of strength in every undertaking.'

3. GEMINI ♊

'Thou Airy Twins hold fast to one another. Display the sign of separation in Divine Duality; cause us to seek and understand both sides of any question. Yet may our human houses never be divided unto their destruction.'

4. CANCER ♋

'O Crab which crawleth in the Ocean of Eternity. Show unto us tenacity and caution, even in the very face of danger; may we ever hold to what is worthy and reject the useless. Seeking in our service to each other our companionship with all Creation.'

5. LEO ♌

'Thou Lionhearted one, with whom all life is faced in fearlessness. Bestow on us the blessing of courageous conduct and decisive action. Fierce are the fires that shine within thy golden eyes. So may we also look upon adversity, yet tremble not before its trials and terrors.'

6. VIRGO ♍

'Thou Virgin of the World retain thy primal purity. O Earth unravished by the hands of man, be thou our true inheritance; Let us rejoice in that which comes to us untarnished. So that the Holy Veil before the Mysteries remains inviolate.'

7. LIBRA ♎

'Thou Balance holding all our happiness within thy scales, let no adverse wind disturb thine equilibrium. May we not be light of weight, nor lacking in the level of our measure; honoured be thine equiponderance. And blessed be the Poising Point of our Creation.'

8. SCORPIO ♏

'O Scorpion by which is signified the Eagle and the Serpent. Sting us into seeking Knowledge; may the Water of the truly Wise refresh our questing souls. And may our search for Hidden Wisdom be rewarded by due revelations of the Holy and Eternal Mysteries.'

9. SAGITTARIUS ⟼

'Thou Archer aiming at Infinity, make Truth thy highest target. Let thy fiery arrows mark the perfect Path for our perception; so may we also aim at ends to be accomplished by our efforts. And swerve not from our course until our ultimate achievement.'

10. CAPRICORNICUS ♑

'O thou Goat of ancient Mysteries, uphold the Light between thy horns. Power of Earth personified, produce in us vitality and vigour; take thou our guilt and let it die within the desert of oblivion. May we falter not upon the precipice of peril, but safely scale the summit of the Holy Mountain.'

11. AQUARIUS ♒

'Thou Airy one by whom is carried water. Worker of the waves and mover of the oceans, may we sail serenely on the seas of consciousness; let us learn to travel with full freedom on the tides of thought. Blessed are the vessels that must bear us, and welcome is the wind that brings us safely into harbour.'

12. PISCES ♓

'Thou Fish that finalize the Cycle of Creation. Out of Oceans we emerged, and into unknown depths we plunge when life is ended; Let our term of Earth-existence serve successfully the ends of Evolution. May we never perish utterly, but be restored to Life again within the Blessed Waters of Regeneration.'

Quite a great deal can be done with chants like this. They may be taken in sections person by person, worked in responses choir-fashion, or done entirely by one individual, the rest coming in with a 'SO MOTE IT BE' in between sections. Every Circle ought to have its regular chants to fall back on for achieving Inner conditions of consciousness suitable for whatever rite is being worked. They are a *sine qua non* of good Circle-construction, and should never be neglected. Listening to them, or other ritual items on tape is helpful for becoming familiar with them by rote, but of course nothing can possibly supersede their practical use by living souls in company with one another.

Now enough Ritual groundwork and material has been given for anyone with real will and ability to build up their own Circle-system. Everything leads to something else, and no individual efforts, however crude or inexpert, can be entirely wasted. It is better to start in simple straightforward ways that establish a really sound Nucleus for any Circle of Cosmos, than try and build up some showy but ramshackle affair that falls to pieces with the first push from Inner Powers.

One thing is quite certain. Any attempt at forming a ritualized Circle-Cross will very definitely be investigated and tested out by Inner Ones of Power for their own reasons. Some Circles may survive this treatment, and others not. Everything depends upon the motivation of the Circle-members, and their relationships with each other. If these are properly balanced and constituted, the Circle will live to take its place in the Great Plan of Cosmos, and become a vital part of what we might term the 'Divine Body'. Otherwise – it is better for an imperfect and faulty Circle to be broken up for re-use elsewhere. Nothing is gained by trying to maintain unhealthy organisms which refuse to reconstitute themselves into better spiritual structures when afforded opportunities for doing so.

The life of every Circle must come, as with individuals, from inside itself. Once the Cosmic Entity appertaining to a Circle makes itself felt among the human members, they will more or less automatically begin to 'pick up' all sorts of 'inside information' and experience for themselves enough to realize that they are dealing with positive Inner realities, and not mere figments of their wishful thinking or misguided imagination. To reach this state of awareness may take years, or even lifetimes. Nevertheless, it will not be very long in Earth-time before conscientious Ritualists feel quite sure that they are working for very genuine reasons connected with Inner Cosmic Life, and not solely for the sake of amusing fun and games.

Strictly speaking, Quarterly Rites should be the culminating points of every minor rite worked by all members of Circles for themselves during the past Season. If nobody has done anything very much, the Quarterlies can scarcely be very potent affairs. Therefore, those who only intend to treat Quarterlies as a sort of social occasion with spiritual side-effects, have no legitimate complaint if they find no sort of fulfilment in the ceremonies. No-one in their right mind would expect instant oaks from fresh-planted acorns, and all souls considering Cosmic-Circle working should remember this vital point. Spiritual seeds take even more time than physical ones to mature, and unless we recognize this fact, we shall live in constant disappointment instead of confident faith. Once the Quarterly Rites have been kept going for a few Earthly Seasons, they will begin to show Inner results sure enough, but none need demand ridiculous miracles from the same Natural Life and its Laws Which maintains all Cosmos in Creative Circles.

What we are really doing with our Quarterly and other Ritual activities is to promote ourselves from pawns to players on the checker-board of Cosmos. This is the pattern presented to every neophyte who enters a Lodge. The choice is ours. Either we are completely pushed around from square to square, or we learn to participate at least to some extent in the game, and develop the art of Circling with Will. We conform with the squares, or draw our own designs with the Compasses. Which? Let every single soul decide their ultimate spiritual Destiny AS THEY WILL. There is no other Way ahead to Wherever we intend ourselves to:

BE WHAT WE WILL BECOME

in

PEACE PROFOUND.

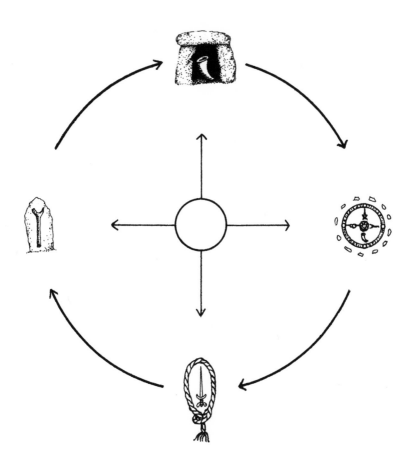

Lightning Source UK Ltd.
Milton Keynes UK
UKHW03f1041020418
320391UK00002B/419/P

9 781908 011800